A Biblical Guide
to the End *of the* World

A Biblical Guide
to the End of the World

DAVID MURDOCH

RESOURCE *Publications* · Eugene, Oregon

A BIBLICAL GUIDE TO THE END OF THE WORLD

Copyright © 2022 David Murdoch. All rights reserved. Except for brief quotations in critical publications or reviews, no part of this book may be reproduced in any manner without prior written permission from the publisher. Write: Permissions, Wipf and Stock Publishers, 199 W. 8th Ave., Suite 3, Eugene, OR 97401.

Resource Publications
An Imprint of Wipf and Stock Publishers
199 W. 8th Ave., Suite 3
Eugene, OR 97401

www.wipfandstock.com

PAPERBACK ISBN: 978-1-6667-4530-6
HARDCOVER ISBN: 978-1-6667-4531-3
EBOOK ISBN: 978-1-6667-4532-0

FEBRUARY 3, 2025 11:36 AM

"NLT" signifies scripture quotation taken from the *Holy Bible*, New Living Translation, copyright © 1996, 2004, 2015 by Tyndale House Foundation. Used by permission of Tyndale House Publishers, Inc., Carol Stream, Illinois 60188. All Rights Reserved.

"ESV" signifies scripture quotation is from the ESV®Bible (The Holy Bible, English Standard Version®), copyright © 2001 by Crossway, a publishing ministry of Good News Publishers. Used by permission. All rights reserved.

I dedicate this book to the Lord God—these are the first fruits from his wonderful counsel, teaching and help, without which this book would be nothing.

"And so I tell you, keep on asking, and you will receive what you ask for. Keep on seeking, and you will find. Keep on knocking, and the door will be opened to you. For everyone who asks, receives. Everyone who seeks, finds. And to everyone who knocks, the door will be opened." *NLT*

—Lord Jesus of Nazareth

"Thus says the Lord who made the earth, the Lord who formed it to establish it—the Lord is his name: Call to me and I will answer you, and will tell you great and hidden things that you have not known." *ESV*

—The Lord through Jeremiah

Contents

Introduction | *xv*

Important Points | 1

    The End of Our History is a Hebrew Wedding | 1
    Jesus? Or Yeshua? Or Who? | 1
    Jesus, Holy Spirit, and Father? Isn't There One God? | 2
    You Will Need a Bible—Paper or Online | 3
    The Bible—Errors or No Errors? | 4
    Bible Linearity and Typical Prophecy | 4
    The Book of Revelation is the Key to the End Times | 6
    The Seven Major Time Blocks | 7

Prologue | 8

    A Message to the Churches: Revelation 1, Revelation 2, Revelation 3 | 8
        The Throne in Heaven—Come and Meet God | 10

Time Block 1A | 12

    The Beginning of the End: Revelation 12:5 | 12
        The End is Nigh! Or is it? | 12
        The Jewish Wedding | 14
        The Parable of the Wedding Feast: Matthew 22:1–6 | 16
        Jesus's Birth, Ministry, Death, and Resurrection | 17
        Truly, Truly I Tell You, This Generation Will Not Pass . . . | 18

Welcome to Revelation 12 | 19

Timeline Segment Summary: Time Block 1A | 20

Time Block 2A | 21

Dark Times and the Dawning of the Modern Age: Revelation 2, Revelation 3, Revelation 5, Revelation 6:1–4 | 21

Early History and the Start of Modern Times | 21

Jesus is the Lamb of God | 23

The Four Horsemen, Part One | 23

    The First Seal | 24

    The Second Seal | 25

Destruction of the Temple | 25

First Angel of Revelation 14 | 26

Timeline Segment Summary: Time Block 2A | 27

Time Block 2B | 28

The Formation of Today's Modern World: Revelation 2, Revelation 3, Revelation 6:5–11 | 28

The Four Horsemen: Part Two | 28

    The Third Seal | 29

    The Fourth Seal | 30

    The Four Horses—A Conclusion to be Drawn | 30

ADxxxx? When do Modern Times Begin? | 31

How Long Have We Got? Give a Date! | 33

The Wedding Feast Parable Continues | 34

What Sort of People Will Dominate the World? | 35

A Comment About Luke 21:7–36 | 36

Timeline Segment Summary: Time Block 2B | 37

Interlude | 38

Important Points About the Sun, Moon, and Stars | 38

Time Block 3A | 42

Jesus is Revealed—the Day of the Lord: Revelation 6:12–17, Revelation 7 | 42

    Warning! A Second Coming of Christ | 42

    The Elect | 44

    Let's Talk About Rapture | 46

        Be Ready! | 47

        If You Lose Your Life, You Will Keep It | 48

There Are at Least Three Gatherings | 49

    Other Passages to Consider for Rapture | 50

    Timeline Segment Summary: Time Block 3A | 52

Time Block 3B | 54

Destruction of the Status Quo: Revelation 8, Revelation 12:7–12 | 54

    Whatever World-wide Cultures Exist—They End Here | 54

    Yichud—or Period Alone | 55

    Revelation Continues with the Trumpets | 55

    The Second Angel of Revelation 14 | 57

    Timeline Segment Summary—Time Block 3B | 58

Time Block 4A | 59

Terror One—The Destroyer's Locust Army: Revelation 9:1–11 | 59

    The Start of the Terrors | 59

    The Destroyer (A.K.A. Abaddon)—Terror One | 60

    Timeline Segment Summary: Time Block 4A | 61

Time Block 4B | 62

Terror Two—Gigantic Attack: Revelation 9:13–21, Revelation 13:1–4 | 62

    The Second Terror Follows | 62

    Who is the Unfortunate Remainder of Mankind? | 63

The Beginnings of the Fourth Kingdom | 65

Timeline Segment Summary: Time Block 4B | 66

Interlude—A Brief Explanation of The Beasts | 67

The Angel of Death, Beast from the Sea, Beast from the Earth, Abomination of Desolation | 67

The Angel of The Pit (Abyss) "Abaddon" or Angel of Death | 67

Beast from the Sea: Revelation 13:1–3 | 67

The Beast from the Earth: Revelation 13:11–14 | 71

The Abomination of Desolation: Matthew 24:15 | 71

The Dragon: Revelation 12:3 | 72

Time Block 4C–4E | 75

Terror Two and Three—The Beast Kingdom and Its Ruler: A Complete Overview | 75

The Signs and Times of the Final World Order | 75

Daniel, Revelation, and the Time Periods | 77

Time Block 4C | 79

Terror Two Continues—A New King Rules: Revelation 11:1–14, Revelation 12:6, Revelation 12:13–16, Revelation 13:5–6, Revelation 17:1–10, 18 | 79

The New World Kingdom and a New Babylon | 79

The Third Temple Must Exist | 81

The Two Witnesses and the Little Horn | 81

Timeline Segment Summary: Time Block 4C | 83

Time Block 4D | 84

Terror 3—Mark of the Beast and Abomination of Desolation: Revelation 13:7–10, Revelation 13:11–18, Revelation 17:12–18, Revelation 18 | 84

A Time Given By Jesus (Spoken by Daniel) | 84

A Terrible Time for All Who Follow God, and For All That Don't | 85

The Number of the Beast: 666 | 86

　　　Timeline Segment Summary: Time Block 4D | 87

Time Block 4E | 89

　　Terror 3 Continues—Massive Angelic War on Earth: Revelation 14:14–16, Revelation 15, Revelation 16 | 89

　　　The Massive War and the Seven Bowls | 89

　　　The End of Terror Three | 90

　　　The Archangel Michael Rises | 91

　　　Harvesting the Earth—Or Post Tribulation Rapture | 93

　　　Why 30 Days for the Seven Bowls? | 94

　　　Timeline Segment Summary: Time Block 4E | 95

Time Block 5A | 96

　　Jesus Returns—The Day of the Lord: Revelation 14:17–20, Revelation 16:17–21, Revelation 19 | 96

　　　This is not Judgment Day | 96

　　　Darkened Sun, Dark Moon | 98

　　　Is it a Day? Maybe, Maybe Not—But Focus on the Message | 98

　　　The Gathering of the 144 000 | 99

　　　The Feast of Flesh | 100

　　　Satan, The Beast, The False Prophet | 100

　　　The Wedding Feast | 101

　　　Timeline Segment Summary: Time Block 5A | 102

Time Block 5B | 103

　　The 44 Day Transition—Or the Day of the Lord Continues: Revelation 20:1–6 | 103

　　　Satan is Taken Out of the Equation | 103

　　　Beast Kingdom Leaders and Heavenly Associates (Fallen Angels) Imprisoned | 104

　　　The First Resurrection | 105

Language Purified | 107

Life During the Transition, and After the Day of the Lord | 107

Timeline Segment Summary: Time Block 5B | 108

Time Block 6A | 109

The 1 000 Year Reign of Christ on Earth: Revelation 20:4–6 | 109

Jesus Christ on Earth in Jerusalem | 109

The Reinstatement of a Temple | 111

The 144 000 Elect, Saints and More | 113

Sheep and Goats—Salvation through Good Works? | 114

Terrible Flesh Eating Madness Disease? | 116

Timeline Segment Summary: Time Block 6A | 117

Time Block 6B | 119

Satan Released to Gather Followers. Instant Defeat: Revelation 20:7–10 | 119

Amazing Non-Battle | 119

Timeline Segment Summary: Time Block 6B | 121

Time Block 7A | 122

The Judgment of All—The Final Day of the Lord: Revelation 20:11–15 | 122

The End! This *is* Judgment Day | 122

Goodbye Spacetime | 123

Everyone Gets a New Eternal Body | 123

The Parable of the Wedding Feast Ends | 124

A Quick Note on Damnation | 126

Who Does the Judging? | 127

Judgment Process | 127

The Book of Life is the Key | 128

Timeline Segment Summary: Time Block 7A | 130

Time Block 7B | 131

Eternity: Revelation 21, Revelation 22 | 131

Eternal Epilogue | 131
No More Sin | 132
Lake of Fire (Second Death) and Outer Darkness | 132
Who Wants Eternity? It'll be *Boring*! | 133
New Heavens, New Earth, and New Jerusalem | 134
The Tree of Life | 135
Timeline Segment Summary: Time Block 7B | 137

Conclusion | 138

What to do and Where are We? | 138
A Final Word | 140

Appendix A | 143

Do You Know Jesus? | 143

Appendix B | 145

Who is the "I AM"? | 145

Bibliography | 147

Introduction

Use Thought, Rebuke Stubborn Pride

Final Words

And so, dear friends, while you are waiting for these things to happen, make every effort to be found living peaceful lives that are pure and blameless in his sight.

And remember, our Lord's patience gives people time to be saved. This is what our beloved brother Paul also wrote to you with the wisdom God gave him — speaking of these things in all of his letters. Some of his comments are hard to understand, and those who are ignorant and unstable have twisted his letters to mean something quite different, just as they do with other parts of Scripture. And this will result in their destruction. You already know these things, dear friends. So be on guard; then you will not be carried away by the errors of these wicked people and lose your own secure footing. Rather, you must grow in the grace and knowledge of our Lord and Savior Jesus Christ.

All glory to him, both now and forever! Amen. NLT — 2 Peter 3:14–18

MODERN MEDIA IS A strange environment; full of ideas, notions, and peoples' self-important and self-serving beliefs. It is difficult to sort out truth from distraction, real from fake. It is a fertile breeding ground for various conspiracy theories whose followings are widespread, with human nature typically trusting whatever reasoning is behind the theories, without checking solid, neutral sources.

Introduction

We want to believe because it is exciting or it panders to our own beliefs; or because we have a sense of belonging, and there is nothing quite like being "right" amongst others who will agree with you.

However, unlike modern media, the Bible is bedrock. The writings it contains today are remarkably similar to the incredibly old texts found in caves in deserts in and around Israel[1]. This makes it quite unapproachable in many ways, because unlike the modern media we see or watch, the Bible does not change to fit our desires. It remains almost entirely as it was, no matter how many followers it might generate or lose, or how many likes people do or do not give it.

With this in mind, we are warned by God (in the Bible) to expect many false prophets to rise up during the end times to mislead and to cause people to stumble. We, as a human race, love disasters. We have our interest piqued by them, so there is a market for all and sundry to provide their own version of upcoming oppressive events.

What makes false prophets so dangerous is that there is often quite a lot of truth in what they say, just as Satan himself spoke truths to Jesus when he tempted Jesus in the desert. These truths resonate with us and our already heightened state of interest, and we believe the rest of what is said must also be true, right? The worst kind of falsehood is that which hides between many layers of righteous truth.

So then, what of this reference guide to the End Times? Is there a hidden agenda? To make you stumble? To push forward opinions in pride-driven passion? Think and study! This calls for wisdom, discernment, thought on your part, and definitely prayer for the truth to be shown. I approached this study as humbly as I could, but I am still human so don't trust me blindly, as I am flawed. Read the passages I show, in the places I believe they reside, and use thought, prayer, and understanding.

The process I went through to create this timeline was simple, yet difficult to adhere to. I would seek out the references to the events laid out in the Bible from the Bible itself, and not wander too far off that source. The first few passes through my journey on this study were almost entirely that concept, and I listened to the Holy Spirit as he guided me through the very twisty, very deep thread of wisdom in God's Word. The Bible states this idea in 1 Corinthians 2:11–13:

> For who knows a person's thoughts except the spirit of that person, which is in him? So also, no one comprehends the thoughts of God

1. Wikipedia, *Isaiah Scroll*

Introduction

except the Spirit of God. Now we have received not the spirit of the world, but the Spirit who is from God, that we might understand the things freely given us by God. And we impart this in words not taught by human wisdom but taught by the Spirit, interpreting spiritual truths to those who are spiritual. ᴱˢⱽ

Here then is my own fallibility, for I *cannot* remove from my mind what I have heard and understood from my culture, upbringing, and interests. The same weighting of ideas will apply to you, too. Whatever you currently believe to be true will be the concrete foundation from which you will read this study. Sometimes, the content of this study might crack your foundation—then take the time to ponder, research, and check the word in the Bible and in legitimate, neutral Bible studies.

Topics such as "Rapture," "666," "The Beast," "Daniel's Weeks," and what I previously understood about the nature of our Lord Jesus's return remain in my mind, weighting and blurring my response to the Holy Spirit's teachings and guidance. This is like the Holy Spirit providing instructions at me from the bank of a rushing river–telling me how to paddle to shore. All I can do is paddle how I remember to paddle, try to hear over the sounds of the waters all around me, trust that the Spirit on the river bank is 100 percent correct at all times, and that I am going to go in the right direction if I follow him across this turbulence.

With this in mind, the final few passes through this study were a sanity check using three pillars, as they were called by my pastor. These are: Tradition (i.e. the historical context of the passages I had been guided to, that I was not aware of); Scripture (i.e. all ideas must come from, and point back to, the complete Bible); the Holy Spirit (i.e. inspiration and direction from God himself). Using these three checks and balances, I refined and honed the study with each pass, hopefully diluting David Murdoch's will accordingly.

We cling to what we believe, and I know many people will come to this timeline looking for confirmation of their beliefs rather than discovering what God has laid out in the Bible. All I can say is: do not accept what I say without thought. Do not reject what I say with your pride.

Throughout this study, I took onboard what the Bible writes about "wisdom from above" in the book of James. I have no personal ambition; rather, I am hopeful that God's true plan is explained and understood. That way, you'll know the complex end, what is happening, and what to do about it.

Introduction

James also tells us to ask God for wisdom, and once asked, to have faith that God will show you the wisdom. We are not supposed to ask our favorite muse (perhaps the person we feel will give us the right answers and agree with us), whether they think God's answer is right, for to do so will have us pushed around like rudderless ships. I resisted this as best I could, and I can tell you this was the greatest struggle in writing this guide, for some things that I received from God did not match what I had heard from others. What then? The answer is to swallow pride, to expect rebuke, and put on paper what the Lord illuminated in his Word, through his Spirit.

However, remember I am not a special person God has revealed some secret mystery to, that no-one else has discerned or been led by the Spirit to write. No, I am simply illuminating what is already known as it is written in the Bible, and assembling it to assist understanding.

How then do I know it is the Holy Spirit, and not Satan, whispering? A simple test is this: the wisdom and knowledge granted must agree with all parts of the Bible, and God, in context, without bending it to fit my personal will. It should not jar awkwardly and other Christians should receive similar wisdom, or illumination by revelation. My pastor enlightened me to the fact that the Holy Spirit is not a Spirit of Confusion, but of Truth. This is stated in 1 Corinthians 14:31–33 by Paul inspired by God. What I have discerned should not generate confusion, but instead understanding and a need to go and check for yourself. It should fit those three "pillars"–Traditional context, Scriptural pointing, and Holy Spirit agreement.

This guidance from the Holy Spirit *should not* pander to your ambitions and desires, or want to force people to fit the "letter of the law", as Paul says in 2 Corinthians 3:5–6:

> Not that we are sufficient in ourselves to claim anything as coming from us, but our sufficiency is from God, who has made us sufficient to be ministers of a new covenant, not of the letter but of the Spirit. For the letter kills, but the Spirit gives life. ᴱˢⱽ

Finally, the message should not appease your comfortable way of life at the cost of the truth from God. Let me just clarify that–anyone who reads the Bible knows that it can be a great source of comfort, but it has many emotions, and during the end times there is not a lot of comfort to be had for a lot of people. It is a heavy message, and a lot of tribulation to come.

So then, I hope that puts you in the right frame of mind for studying this guide. It isn't perfect, I am not perfect, but I have rested heavily on the Bible and the Holy Spirit. May he be glorified, not me! Amen.

Important Points

The End of Our History is a Hebrew Wedding

During the gathering and sorting of the many Bible verses and scripture of the end times, I discovered the end of our history began as an ancient Jewish Wedding ceremony between Christians (the Bride), and our groom, Jesus. This sounds bizarre when you hear this, but it turns out that Jesus himself, along with the Bible, alluded to this in parables and comments made.

The symbolism and stages of a Jewish or Hebrew wedding are important to understand, especially in applying these stages to the End of the World. With that in mind, for those who have not seen or heard about Jewish Weddings, I recommend researching the stages of such a ceremony. They differ quite a lot from the standard Western wedding I have experienced in my life, so your own culture may also differ significantly from the context of a wedding described in the Bible.

In this study I will highlight each stage of the Jewish wedding to show how it relates to the periods of time we are discussing.

Jesus? Or Yeshua? Or Who?

When Jesus was born, around 5 BC, his name was not Jesus! A quick online search of "how Yeshua became Jesus" will help you understand this. However, as God the Father caused our language to disperse and become confused during the Babel period, I'm sure he is fine with those who know the name Jesus, calling his son "Jesus." After all, our language teaches us this name, but in our hearts, we know whom we are referring to.

Therefore, throughout this study I will use the name Jesus as being the Son of Man, God's only son and part of the one God in three aspects. You should also be aware, in the future, Jesus gets a new name that the whole of humanity will know. We will all praise him using that one name.

Jesus, Holy Spirit, and Father? Isn't There One God?

For those who are not Christian, and indeed for those who are, it can be very hard for our human minds to conceive how three seemingly separate entities can be one. This has led to some Muslims and Jehovah's Witnesses to believe that Christians worship multiple gods—and then they get upset because God tells us very plainly and clearly that he is the ONLY God! Trust me when I say this: we as Christians do worship just *One Living God*. But how that one mighty God decides to interact with our reality is up to him, not our limited minds—and he chose to do so through a physical human body (Jesus), his Spirit (Holy Spirit) and himself (The Father, who our minds cannot comprehend—hence Jesus, who we can relate to).

Throughout this study, you will see all three aspects of God in play. Sometimes at the same time such is his mighty nature; he can do this, whereas we can't. What we can do is think of ourselves in this way: we have an immortal Soul and Spirit and a mortal Body, yet we are one being.

Even if you are not a spiritual person, you can understand a philosophical separation of mind and body, where the body is autonomous and its own master, and so is the mind, and yet this forms a symbiotic person. Why, therefore, should there be difficulty understanding one God in three parts?

If I asked you to draw three circles on a page, I would be almost 100 percent certain you'd end up with three circles on a page! That's our typical human mind response. Try drawing three circles right now and see what you draw.

Tell me, who would draw three circles directly on top of each other, so they look like one circle? One above the other? This is how three are one. Three circles, but one circle.

We look at Jesus, the Father, and the Holy Spirit and can't see how they can be one; to us they look like three distinct circles on the page because our simple dimensional thinking restricts us. But they *are* one! Our way of understanding does not limit God himself.

Important Points

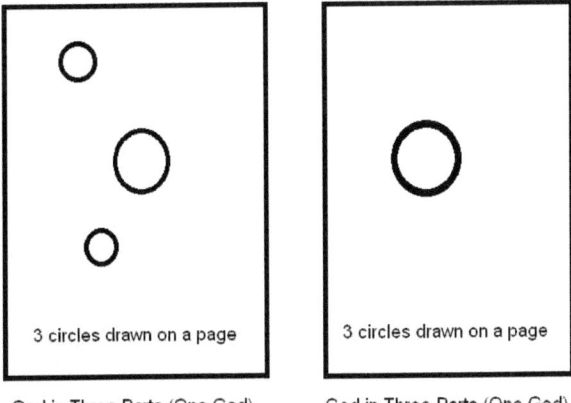

Father, Jesus, Holy Spirit: God. One entity, three distinct parts, linked as a whole in a way that is mysterious to us.

You Will Need a Bible—Paper or Online

Access to a Bible will greatly help you in this study. Without a Bible it will be hard to get the depth of the wisdom provided. You can either purchase one, or just search each passage freely on the internet as there are now amazing resources at our fingertips. If however, due to an oppressive regime or fear of attack, you are unable to get internet access or a Bible, attempt to contact the Bible League Canada[1] at +1-800-363-9673, Fax +1-905-319-0484, email: ministry@bibleleague.ca; or Shareword Global at +1-888-482-4253, email: info@sharewordglobal.com and they will help you.

If you simply don't care to read the Bible, all you'll get from this study is a weird and brief overview—like one of those movie trailers from Hollywood where they show all the good bits but you don't really know if the movie is worth the money. You could easily speed read through this study within a day, but then you might as well turn to page 141 and look at the summary table which will tell you all you need to know at that level.

With all the free Bibles in so many languages and styles online, the Western world has no excuse for avoiding the passages I highlight, apart from apathy or not setting aside time to study.

Here are a couple I grabbed from the internet for you:

1. https://bibleleague.ca/contact/

Matthew 27:46–47:

> "And about the ninth hour Jesus cried out with a loud voice, saying, "Eli, Eli, lema sabachthani?" that is, "My God, my God, why have you forsaken me?" And some of the bystanders, hearing it, said "This man is calling Elijah." ESV

Psalm 22:1:

> "My God, my God, why have you forsaken me? Why are you so far from saving me, from the words of my groaning?" ESV

That took me about 30 seconds to find each one online. "Matthew" and "Psalm" would be the book (or scroll), the first number is then the chapter (27) and then the verses (46–47) to read from that chapter (e.g., Matthew 27:46–47 will give you two verses 46 and 47, from chapter 27, of Matthew).

The Bible—Errors or No Errors?

I am one of those Christians who thinks the Bible's messages are truth, and any errors or additions that have come later do not change the message. If there are problems, they are due to translation difficulties or our way of thinking trapped in our basic senses, stuck in our limited universe, not approaching God's way of thinking (see three circles previously).

The clash of science and Bible illumination is normal, as God tells us we will *never* comprehend him and his ways. Never. He is not constrained by his creation like we are and can do anything he chooses. Weird things do happen, and a culture that was all about recording events and ensuring accurate *written* copies were preserved wrote about these in scripture, which became part of the Bible.

Bible Linearity and Typical Prophecy

Now a word about Bible Prophecy that is important to understand: you should not expect perfect linearity—the march of time does not bind God. It is clear he exists outside and through the space-time bubble he created. He gave prophets messages and visions as he saw fit, and it is foolish to believe these read like a cheap novel. No, the Bible jumps thousands of years in one punctuation period. It can jump back to the beginning, or it can

Important Points

jump forwards many years to the end. It is very much like a story that has a single, long arc, but each episode or chapter can be past, present, or future, or all of them at once. However, the single thread running through the story is continuous and unchanged.

The Bible is a living Word of God, and will speak to you personally, as well as in the grand scale of human history. The Holy Spirit will illuminate what you need to know through the words in the Bible. If you have ever read the Parable of the Talents (Matthew 25:14-30) you will understand; this is classic multi-meaning wisdom, where you will get different inspiration from it depending on the state of your life and where you are.

You also need to be aware of a term called "Typical Prophecy" where warnings and prophecy apply repeatedly through history, and can still be relevant for the future too—this is like a pattern or a template reapplied many times. This makes it hard to understand which part goes where; but again, ask for wisdom, then meditate on what you receive, read the Bible again, and repeat as necessary.

Babylon is one such repetitive term, illustration, and pronoun. God uses the Babylon pattern to mean the same sort of society or city-like state again and again, and not necessarily the one Babylon we know of that physically existed.

Another example is the phrase the Day of the Lord. There are three contextual Day of the Lord moments in the end times, and it stands for a period of time when a great holy and mighty change occurs due to God himself coming to us and doing powerful, world-changing things. Think of a big global reset for the three Day of the Lords we will be looking at: the revealing of Christ in Time Block 3A, the return of Christ for a thousand year reign in Time Block 5A onwards, and the end of our spacetime in Time Block 7A.

Of course, our own thoughts will also fit things to the words we read; this is our typical way of being. With that in mind, it is good to relax, don't be passionate or certain that you are right and check what you think you've understood. If "the Holy Spirit is not a spirit of confusion," the truth will shine amongst all those listening openly to the Spirit. Remember 1 Corinthians 14:31-33: the Holy Spirit has got the Father's good will to teach us, so why would he confuse us? Confusion belongs to the other camp and is an effective weapon. See the world for many examples of end-time confusion, no doubt whispered by Satan to derail as many as he can in the time left.

A Biblical Guide to the End of the World

The Book of Revelation is the Key to the End Times

It is important to state that the Book of Revelation is all you need. Why do I say that? Because God's Word tells us so, right at the start of Revelation:

> The revelation of Jesus Christ, which God gave him to show to his servants the things that must soon take place. He made it known by sending his angel to his servant John, who bore witness to the word of God and to the testimony of Jesus Christ, even to all that he saw. ESV

Revelation writings are the things that soon take place. You can also translate soon as *suddenly* or *quickly*. This is more likely, given the time between God revealing this to John, through to today and our awaiting the revealing of Jesus to the whole modern world.

Therefore, Revelation is the foundation of future events that we are to study. There will be other passages in the Bible that point to the events in Revelation, but using what we know in Revelation as grounding, we can see if the past prophecies are fulfilled or still outstanding and waiting their appointed time. Some material in Biblical scripture (e.g., Isaiah, Daniel, and Ezekiel) have not come to fruition yet, even though written thousands of years ago.

Today, there are hot topics Christians and others are excitedly waiting for; Christ's Return, The Rapture, the Day of the Lord, The Beast Empire and the Number of the Beast - 666, Christ's 1 000-year Reign, Judgment Day, etc. This emotional excitement starts to read too much into Bible passages that may or may not confirm their thoughts. However, the Book of Revelation is a guide to where these passages actually apply, and what may have been misinterpreted.

Jesus and his angel spoke and presented the revelation to John, and John faithfully recorded all that he saw and heard. It is what God told and showed him. Therefore, we cannot argue that Revelation is wrong, because then we will be saying that Jesus failed to get the message to us. And if you think that, you might as well stop reading this guide as it will be a waste of your time.

Know in your heart, no matter how odd Revelation seems to you it is truth, but it is difficult to understand. Think of Revelation as a poetic guide to what is going to happen, not a literal instruction manual.

Important Points

The Seven Major Time Blocks

When traveling through the complex flow of the End Times, I created a long timeline map of the events to help see the appropriate Bible passages in the right place in time. However, when I printed off the complete timeline from beginning to end it was longer than my kitchen table!

I realized that there needed to be individual chapters that dealt with and explained the obvious chunks that form the whole. So, this led me to split up the end times into significant "Time Blocks" as I call them. This helps track backwards and forwards, and each chapter has a summary of scripture that forms the block we are discussing.

Prologue

A Message to the Churches: Revelation 1, Revelation 2, Revelation 3

Before we start looking at our future in-depth, we have a small prologue at the very start of Revelation to study. This introduction is about who gave the prophecy to the Apostle John, as well as some important messages to the seven churches of those days that are still relevant to us. Here are some introductory verses from Revelation 1:4–6:

> John to the seven churches that are in Asia:
> Grace to you and peace from him who is and who was and who is to come, and from the seven spirits who are before his throne, and from Jesus Christ the faithful witness, the firstborn of the dead, and the ruler of kings on earth.
> To him who loves us and has freed us from our sins by his blood and made us a kingdom, priests to his God and Father, to him be glory and dominion forever and ever. Amen.[ESV]

The early verses of Revelation paint an interesting picture, aimed at us in the time before the end, and produce the following points we will study throughout this Time Block investigation:

* God the Father is the One "who is and who was and who is to come." This speaks of the eternity of God, in that He covers all instances of when.
* Jesus is the faithful witness. This tells us his time spent in his ministry on Earth back in the Gospel days were truthful and can be trusted.
* Jesus is the Firstborn of the dead; the first risen, or the New Adam. We touch on this concept later in this study when we come to the First Resurrection.

Prologue

- Jesus is the King of Kings, which points to the ancient prophecies of a conquering Messiah. Here he will sit as king on the Earth and subdue all other authority under him. This is exactly what the people of Roman occupied Jerusalem were expecting to happen over 2 000 years ago when Jesus came to die for our redemption.
- Jesus is the First, the Last, and the Living (Alpha and Omega and Living God). Note how this relates to the "who is and who was and who is to come," as well as another important point of being the first of the new creation, the last of the old creation (everyone passes through him), and the Living God of both the current and future creations.
- Jesus is coming with the clouds in such a way that every eye will see him, and interestingly all tribes will wail (or mourn) because of Jesus. This happens twice and we will study this in the upcoming Time Blocks.

The first chapter of Revelation draw out all the above. It is to put us into the right frame of mind as we carry on, and these topics will be touched on throughout.

Then, as Jesus delivers the messages for the churches throughout Revelation 2 and 3, he reveals more interesting points for us to study in this book. These are as follows:

- There is a Tree of Life in God's paradise, and those that hold fast to faith and overcome the issues they face, can eat of it.
- There is a second death. This is the lake of fire mentioned further on in Revelation. This means everyone has to die once, and unfortunately, some end up with a second death.
- There are some given the same authority as Jesus during his 1 000-year reign on Earth as the Messiah, to control the wayward nations with a rod of iron.
- There is a Book of Life and, very importantly, you can be blotted out of it through your choice (no one else's).
- Through our patient endurance, Jesus will keep us from the hour of trial that is coming to the whole earth.
- There is a Temple of God, and we can be a pillar or strong leader in it. This cannot be in the eternal Heaven, in the New Jerusalem right at the end of this journey, as we are told there is no temple in Heaven

(see Revelation 21:22), so this must apply to the upcoming 1 000-year reign of Christ coming later in this study.

There are other points you can learn from the messages to the churches, and I recommend you read them all and think about modern life and the Christians you may know, for we all fit some of these churches—hence the warnings.

When you come to Revelation Chapter 4, you have come to a line drawn in the Book of Revelation. What is this line? It is an end to the present tense and a beginning of what is to come.

The Throne in Heaven—Come and Meet God

When I got my Gideon's New Testament at school, one of the first books I read after the Gospels was Revelation. I wanted to see what happened at the end of the story.

Being quite young (about twelve years old), I read to chapter 2, got bored of the messages to the churches as it was not relevant to me at the time, and skipped to Revelation 4. This is where I restarted my young reading, and the words ignited my imagination!

To start with, note at the start of this chapter Jesus states to John: "Come up here, and I will show you what must take place after this."

This means those churches we read of in Chapters 2 and 3 are *this*. They are now, from when the first churches formed many centuries ago, to present day and onwards, until what must take place after "this." We will see that "this" continues throughout Time Block 2B until Jesus is revealed.

We are next introduced to God residing in Heaven in very symbolic and analogous ways. John could only use words and contextual societal descriptions for what his human mind saw.

This is a good point to stop and consider, for the world in which John wrote had no modern relatable technology and not a lot of science to explain things. We really do take for granted our exposure to the vast amounts of imagery and science of the twentieth and twenty-first centuries; so when a person describes a sea of glass like crystal, or a living creature full of eyes, what did he actually see? And what does this actually mean? God presented these scenes to John to relate to John's contextual knowledge of his culture from his time. I will touch on this again later in Time Block 3B.

Prologue

Now that we have done the groundwork, the journey through the distinct Time Blocks starts; we'll travel through the Book of Revelation, referring back to ancient prophecy that either has been, or will be, fulfilled.

Time Block 1A

The Beginning of the End: Revelation 12:5

The Time Block Overview													
The End Begins	Rise of the Modern World		Jesus Revealed [Day of the LORD]		The Three Terrors					Jesus Returns [Day of the LORD]		1 000-Year Reign		Judgment [Day of the LORD] and New Creation
1	2		3		4					5		6		7
A	A	B	A	B	A	B	C	D	E	A	B	A	B	A	B
Jesus's Birth, Teachings, Death, and Resurrection.															

The End is Nigh! Or is it?

In some Western culture movies and comics there is a man wearing a board that has a sign saying, "The End is Nigh!" Typically, everyone ignores him and goes about their business. Well, that warning period actually happened a long, long time ago, before Jesus was born. The truth is we are in the end already! The sign the man is wearing should simply say "The End Is."

You may not be aware, or have even considered, that the Bible is complete and there is *nothing else to be added.* No more prophecy; those days are over. It contains the complete history of man, from beginning to eternity, so there is no need to prophesy about the end anymore, just understand it. It is a finished history book, and we are in it.

Time Block 1A

Here in Time Block 1A is the start of the end, and immediately we have one of those repetitive prophecies—Psalm 102:18–20. Note this Psalm also applies to later when Jesus rules on the Earth.

> "Let this be recorded for future generations, so that a people not yet born will praise the Lord.
> Tell them the Lord looked down from his heavenly sanctuary.
> He looked down to earth from heaven to hear the groans of the prisoners, to release those condemned to die." NLT

God was going to do something due to the groans of prisoners and will release those condemned to die. What did he do? He sent Jesus to free us, as Jesus himself states in Luke 4:18–19 using the segment of Isaiah's prophecy:

> "The Spirit of the Lord is upon me, for he has anointed me to bring Good News to the poor.
> He has sent me to proclaim that captives will be released, that the blind will see, that the oppressed will be set free, and that the time of the Lord's favor has come." NLT

Sometime around 5 BC the Holy Spirit, doing the Father's will, generated a male embryo in Mary in a way we will never understand. This is God's human body, Jesus. Fully man, fully God. You can't take the man out of Jesus, and you can't take God out of Jesus either—three circles combined remember? Take one out and you don't have the One anymore.

Note the important point there—Jesus was begotten from the Father, and indeed was with the Father before he came physically to us as a man. That takes some philosophical thinking, but Jesus tells us this very fact in John 17:1–5 with his own words. See verse 5:

> "Now, Father, bring me into the glory we shared before the world began." NLT

He was with the Father before the world existed. John also points to this in the mighty John 1:1–18, where everything created was made through The Word, and that Word manifested is Jesus—see vs 14:

> "So the Word became human and made his home among us. He was full of unfailing love and faithfulness. And we have seen his glory, the glory of the Father's one and only Son" NLT

Jesus came to tell us the exceedingly "Good News" about an eternal life; to save us, not judge us yet. He came to reconcile us, teach us, and then wipe our rather grubby slate completely clean by being the sacrifice our redemption required, by the Law God imposed upon us and himself.

By Jesus giving up his life we became free, no longer doomed to eternally die under the old Law. This act is marked in the Western Calendar by Easter, based on the old Jewish lunar calendar timing of the Passover festival. The end of his life on a cross was the sacrifice to end all sacrifices.

Interestingly, the Bible goes on to say Jesus preached to the dead in what the Greeks called Hades and the Jewish race called Sheol (which translates as The Grave). When that was complete, he was resurrected to be the first born of the New Creation and showed himself to *many hundreds* of people before returning to the Father's side in Heaven.

Here is the crux you see—if Jesus is the firstborn of the *New Creation* that means the new creation has already started, and the old one is at its end.

Some people, and especially if you exist as a person in a Wi-Fi/internet/fast-paced world of today, have trouble understanding why this end of the old is taking so long, right? Two thousand years and still counting? What's going on? Has God forgotten?

The Bible has an answer for those people—God is kind and wants to save as many people as possible from the end. So, why lose a single soul if it is possible to keep bringing more under his protective wing?

However, this does not go on forever, as the Bible clearly tells us, and this study shows. For now, let us concentrate on the beginning of the end.

The Jewish Wedding

As I stated in my Important Points section, it appears The Father chose to fit the end events to the stages of a Jewish wedding, of the sort you would find 2 000 years ago. It starts with the father of the groom selecting a bride for his son. Well, you know who the Father is, and who the Son is, so then, who is the Bride he selected many years ago?

This is easy to find in the Bible. Should you desire immediate answers, it is:

1. All who have accepted Jesus as their Lord and Savior and are ceremonially washed and prepared for his return, and
2. The city Jerusalem that has been in God's heart for a very, very long time.

Time Block 1A

Yes, a group of people and the new city they ultimately will become part of. Here is a first nugget of wisdom: the Bride is *not* the current Jerusalem. The Bible tells us the Bride Jerusalem comes down from Heaven in a glorious way; our current Jerusalem is destined to disappear along with the present Heavens and Earth, right at the end.

Next, the Groom promises to look after his Bride and pays the bride price; this was to release the Bride from her family, to set her free from her parents' household. Jesus's blood and death has paid this for us. He paid by dying as a perfect sacrifice required by the Law to atone for sins. He set us free of our parents' household, which is Adam and Eve's unfortunate fallen house, now run by Satan.

The Bride also pays her dowry, which seems to be our own lives, bodies, and our self-driven use of both. We must give up our ownership of our bodies to become temples for Christ, our Groom. We promise to keep ourselves in white garments for him, and these white garments are symbolic of keeping ourselves clean. This is very hard to do in this modern self-centered culture of "It is my body and I'll do what I like with it." The dowry price would seem to be: "It was my body, but now I can't do want I want with it. I have given it over."

During the ceremonial steps at the start, there is a cup of wine shared between Bride and Groom. Jesus, who shared a cup of wine at the Last Supper and declared it the New Covenant in his blood, played this out too. This is the shared cup for the Groom, Jesus, and for us, the Bride. Yes, you have to drink that cup. What does that mean? That you accept his spilled blood as a sacrifice to cleanse your slate clean. That cup is realization, repentance, gratitude, trust, and hope and leads us nicely to the other important requirement: a ritual immersion.

The ritual immersion is to cleanse us before the ceremony. John the Baptist did this to our Groom Jesus. Jesus does this to us through the baptism of the Holy Spirit, but this does not negate the need for a physical ceremony for us. Indeed, for a long time I was very confused as to the need to have someone dunk me in water, even though I had accepted Jesus and definitely had the Holy Spirit. It turns out that God wants us to be ritually washed with water. Confused? Here are verses from Acts 10:47–48, where people that had received the Holy Spirit were still baptized with water, and Peter the apostle declares:

> "Can anyone withhold water for baptizing these people, who have received the Holy Spirit just as we have?" And he commanded

them to be baptized in the name of Jesus Christ. Then they asked him to remain for some days. ᴱˢⱽ

Consider a Western marriage: we can be married in the eyes of the law without a Christian ceremony, but it is a requirement that you say your wedding vows before God if you are married in a church. Therefore, we need to fulfill the physical immersion or ritual washing and declare our vows, as it were, at a baptism service. This is part of being prepared as a Bride for Christ's return.

And here is an important question: how to be baptized? You *do* have to be baptized, that's a certainty, but obtaining that pre-requisite cleaning? I received helpful advice from the Holy Spirit while struggling with this which fulfills any ritual water immersion, sprinkling, pouring, or other ritual cleaning ceremonies:

"By acknowledging and accepting Jesus's Sacrifice and wanting to be made new through it."

If in your heart you believe you are being baptized by the service your church offers, don't let the exact details bog you down. God desires your true love and affection, not regimented arguing. He cares about your heart being right in the matter, not a perfected ritual.

Interestingly, we are in the period where we can partake of the Jewish Wedding Ceremony baptism and carry on becoming a complete, fully formed Bride. Later in the End Times, Jesus will be back on Earth baptizing (ritually cleansing) with fire. This is the Rule with a Rod of Iron.

The Parable of the Wedding Feast: Matthew 22:1–6

Following on from the idea that God has set the rhythm of the End Times to a Jewish Wedding, it is also interesting to apply Jesus's parable of the wedding feast. This is played out in Matthew 22. However, for this Time Block 1A the first portion applies, verses 1–6.

Here we have a king calling people who were invited to come to his son's wedding feast. Unfortunately, the people ignore the messengers more than once and even kill the messengers and servants. Keep in mind these were people the king had invited *beforehand* so they were not surprised by the command to come to the feast. This makes it even more sensational that the invited people would resort to killing the servants rather than go.

Time Block 1A

See verses 5-6:

> "But they paid no attention and went off, one to his farm, another to his business, while the rest seized his servants, treated them shamefully, and killed them." ESV

These people existed throughout the Old Testament before Jesus arrived, and in many ways the Israelites and Jewish leaders that were present during Jesus's first appearance had this frame of mind. Historically, they tended to ignore and even kill prophets sent by God to teach the people where they were going wrong, and to give them the often-repeated message "come back to God and enjoy his blessings."

Jesus's Birth, Ministry, Death, and Resurrection

One of the most remarkable prophecies of the ancient times is Isaiah 9:1-6. Here glory fills the land of Galilee, and a Son born that will ultimately have a government and peace that will never end. The Son rules for eternity. Here is verse 6:

> For to us a child is born, to us a son is given; and the government shall be upon his shoulder, and his name shall be called Wonderful Counselor, Mighty God, Everlasting Father, Prince of Peace. ESV

Also, we have Isaiah 12:1-6. This aligns with Jesus's ministry and purpose, along with verse 5 foretelling the work of the Apostles after Jesus's death and resurrection. Here are verses 3-5:

> With joy you will drink deeply from the fountain of salvation! In that wonderful day you will sing: "Thank the Lord! Praise his name! Tell the nations what he has done. Let them know how mighty he is! Sing to the Lord, for he has done wonderful things. Make known his praise around the world." NLT

There is also remarkable prophecy of the entire chapter of Isaiah 53 which describes Jesus's life, suffering and death, and the reason for it.

For the ministry of Jesus and what happened, along with his ultimate death and resurrection, you simply have to read the four Gospels—Matthew, Mark, Luke, and John; the start of the New Testament. This covers the first Time Block 1A and is an important activity to do before you continue in this study.

Also, Psalm 22 is quite an eye opener. Jesus, on the cross, cried out the starting verse of this psalm by King David when he cried the first part:

> My God, my God, why have you abandoned me? ᴺᴸᵀ

Why? If you read all of Psalm 22 you will find the prophecy fulfilled of Jesus suffering for us. The accounts of his crucifixion in the Gospels of Mark and Luke have many parallels with that psalm.

Truly, Truly I Tell You, This Generation Will Not Pass . . .

A sentence Jesus utters to his disciples about two thousand years ago (Matthew 24:34) creates an interesting issue. The English Standard Version translates it as: "Truly, I say to you, this generation will not pass away until all these things take place." ᴱˢⱽ The chapter of Matthew 24 is Jesus foretelling the future, i.e., the End Times.

Clearly Jesus was speaking to a generation that have passed away, and we have not come to the end of this world. The wisdom I understand? There are two overlapping possibilities that could fulfill the words Jesus spoke.

Firstly, there is another translation of *generation*—namely *age*.[1] When we read Matthew 28:18–20, the now resurrected Jesus tells us he will be with us to the end of the age:

> And Jesus came and said to them, "All authority in heaven and on earth has been given to me. Go therefore and make disciples of all nations, baptizing them in the name of the Father and of the Son and of the Holy Spirit, teaching them to observe all that I have commanded you. And behold, I am with you always, to the end of the age." ᴺᴸᵀ

Days of the Lord typically signify Ends of *Ages*, so this would mean all the things coming up in this study, from Time Block 1A to Time Block 7A, will take place and then *the end of this age* will come. Then the new age with a new Heavens and a new Earth begins—our current age being under the influence of Satan.

Alternatively, in context with Jesus talking about things happening in the future to his disciples, who asked, "what sign will signal your return and the end of the world" (or "age"), and Jesus gives them a prologue up to Matthew 24:14 where he then states "…and then the end will come" we have

---

1. See New Living Translation, Second Edition, Pg.594 footnote 24:34

Time Block 1A

a smaller time period. From the time of the Black Sun, Red Moon (Jesus's revealing) to the Day of the Lord (Jesus returns to Earth in force) when all things he mentions in Matthew 24:15–33 have taken place, could be less than, or equal to, one generation. This would coincide with the entire three Terrors (which includes the Beast Kingdom), and the Day of the Lord of Time Block 5A. How long is a generation? Approximately 20–38 years.

Note: it only took 14 years for the Nazi Party to rise to ultimate power in Germany, between 1919 and 1933 after the devastation of World War One. Therefore 20–38 years to rebuild humanity into a single crushing kingdom after the coming global destruction in Time Block 3B is definitely possible.

Welcome to Revelation 12

Without doubt, this is one of the hardest Revelation chapters to work out in terms of temporal positioning within the End Times. For instance, have a read of Revelation 12:1–6 in your bible of choice and you'll read of Jesus's birth shown in symbolism; but his birth in Time Block 1A is mixed in with images that speak to past and upcoming events during John's time. These include Jesus's ascension in Time Block 2A, the place of protection for the chosen Israelites during the first part of the Beast Kingdom in Time Block 4B and 4C, and Jesus's return and rule in Time Block 6A. Here are verses 5–6:

> She gave birth to a male child, one who is to rule all the nations with a rod of iron, but her child was caught up to God and to his throne, and the woman fled into the wilderness, where she has a place prepared by God, in which she is to be nourished for 1,260 days.[ESV]

Remember one of the important points I made at the start of this book: The Bible is not always linear. Here we have future and past mixed together in a way I suspect God's mind may work. Not linear, but everything at once! If it wasn't for the generous wisdom of the Holy Spirit's guidance and eye-opening sessions, I'd be very lost indeed.

For reference for all of Revelation 12, and you'll find deeper studies on this subject I am sure—the woman is Israel, the nation; the child is Jesus; the dragon is Satan who, quite surprisingly, has access to heaven and even stands before God often accusing us day and night. The Stars of Heaven?

Symbolically, they are angels. You will also find stars falling from Heaven earlier or later in other Bible passages which could be angels or more physical things such as meteorites.

Timeline Segment Summary: Time Block 1A

As we go through this book, I will provide a list of the appropriate and important Bible passages for the Time Block we have just discussed. Sometimes there are many to study, sometimes just one or two.

If you wish to go deeper into what was discussed in this section, read all the passages below. Otherwise, just skip to the next section.

* Parable of the wedding feast: Matthew 22:1–6
* The Birth of Christ foretold: Isaiah 9:1–6, Isaiah 11:1–3, Psalm 102:18–22, Micah 5:2–4
* God becomes our Salvation: Isaiah 12:1–6, Isaiah 28:16
* Christ and his sacrifice: Isaiah 53, Revelation 12:5, John 12:31–32, Matthew 20:17–19, Psalm 22, Mark 15:24–32, and Luke 23:34–39

Time Block 2A

Dark Times and the Dawning of the Modern Age:
Revelation 2, Revelation 3, Revelation 5, Revelation 6:1–4

The Time Block Overview						
The End Begins	Rise of the Modern World	Jesus Revealed [Day of the LORD]	The Three Terrors	Jesus Returns [Day of the LORD]	1 000-Year Reign	Judgment [Day of the LORD] and New Creation
1	2	3	4	5	6	7
A	A | B	A | B	A | B | C | D | E	A | B	A | B	A | B

Jesus departs and gifts the Holy Spirit.
AD70: Destruction of the Temple.

Early History and the Start of Modern Times

Right at the end of Time Block 1A, we had a major part of the Jewish Wedding where a cup of wine is shared between Bride and Groom, ready for the Groom to leave to prepare a place in his Father's house for the Bride.

Now, as the Groom departs, he grants his Bride a gift as a promise of his return—precious but not showy. What was that gift that Jesus left us? The Holy Spirit. See John 14:16–17 below for Jesus's mention of the gift he is sending:

> And I will ask the Father, and he will give you another Advocate who will never leave you. He is the Holy Spirit, who leads into all truth. The world cannot receive him, because it isn't looking for

him and doesn't recognize him. But you know him, because he lives with you now and later will be in you.^{NLT}

This is an amazing gift, and for those who may not understand why, you have to look back at the long period of history before Jesus. Then, God only granted his Spirit to a select few—these were mostly Prophets, but there were others too. Therefore, most people relied heavily on those who had heard or were led by God, and the subsequent writings created by the scribes that recorded the details. For all intents, the entire population was without that direct link to God.

What does that gift of the Holy Spirit mean for us today? Now we have access to God's wisdom, fellowship, counsel, and guidance; a whole amazing host of benefits through the worker of God, his Holy Spirit. Just ask, as Jesus tells us, and he will come to you—and the more you listen, the more the Holy Spirit will speak to you. Especially through the words in the Bible.

Continuing with the Jewish Wedding ceremony: after the gift-giving, the Groom then says goodbye to the Bride and promises to come back to complete the ceremony at his father's command. He then returns to his father's house for a short period, while the Bride prepares herself and gets things in order before she will leave it for good.

As the Groom is Jesus, and the father is The Father, a "short period of time" is seemingly not so—indeed, over two thousand long years? I think we can all agree that that is a long time to wait in anticipation. I am reminded though, as I write this, to point you in the direction of a couple of passages from the Bible. Firstly Habakkuk 2:2–3:

> The Lord's Second Reply
> Then the Lord said to me, "Write my answer plainly on tablets, so that a runner can carry the correct message to others. This vision is for a future time. It describes the end, and it will be fulfilled. If it seems slow in coming, wait patiently, for it will surely take place. It will not be delayed."^{NLT}

And secondly 2 Peter 3:8–9:

> But you must not forget this one thing, dear friends: A day is like a thousand years to the Lord, and a thousand years is like a day. The Lord isn't really being slow about his promise, as some people think. No, he is being patient for your sake. He does not want anyone to be destroyed, but wants everyone to repent. ^{NLT}

Time Block 2A

Jesus is the Lamb of God

After his victory on the cross, and his returning back to his father's house via the ascension, we now see a transition in Heaven. This is all of Revelation 5. Here is a short highlight, verses 6–8:

> Then I saw a Lamb that looked as if it had been slaughtered, but it was now standing between the throne and the four living beings and among the twenty-four elders. He had seven horns and seven eyes, which represent the sevenfold Spirit of God that is sent out into every part of the earth. He stepped forward and took the scroll from the right hand of the one sitting on the throne. And when he took the scroll, the four living beings and the twenty-four elders fell down before the Lamb . . .^{NLT}

We now see Jesus as being the symbolic mighty and wise slaughtered Lamb of God that took away our sins, but also as the only one in Creation worthy of *taking* an important scroll off the Father seated on the throne. To be able to take something out of the right hand of a person seated on a throne shows us something undeniable: who would dare, or would even be able to do so, in the context of John's time? Where kings had ultimate authority over their subjects? This shows us who Jesus is.

He takes the scroll with the seven seals, and receives power, wealth, wisdom, might, honor, glory, and blessings. All these things are due to God, and here the Lamb of God has the same. Indeed, in this transition of Jesus, every single creature gives honor, blessing, glory, and might to he who sits on the throne (the Father) and to the Lamb (Jesus) as equal—remember the three circles, they are separate but one.

This scroll starts the countdown to the Groom's revealing to gather his bride, and to end this modern world.

The Four Horsemen, Part One

After Revelation 5, and the Lamb of God's acceptance, we come to the birth pangs of the end. The timely and painful contractions. Jesus opens the seals of the scroll he took, one after another, and the first four broken seals produce four horses and riders.

The Four Horsemen of the Apocalypse is a well-known idea in the Western World. I grew up with the concept that there would be these four signifiers of the End of the World, and that they would all come together as an End Times event—like a giant show of might as they all ride in, and the end follows swiftly. However, this is a distortion and a corruption of time taken to suit what we believe happens, rather than the slow revealing and increase to breaking point over many centuries.

Jesus tells us many times that he is coming back suddenly, swiftly, and taking those that aren't ready by surprise. But Jesus (or his angel) is telling John in Revelation 6 about a build-up—a series of widespread descriptions of the world that ultimately leads to the Revealing of the Lamb (which is Time Block 3A in this study).

We may spend our days looking for these signs of the Four Horsemen, obsessing over when Jesus is coming back, when in truth we are living in, and have lived, almost *all* of those signifiers already! With the exception of one, which I will talk about in Time Block 2B to follow.

So what of the Horses and Riders that come with every seal broken?

The First Seal

A White Horse with a rider having a bow, given a crown.

The color white is associated with purity and holiness in the Bible, so it has to follow that this rider is holy and pure. Also, this rider goes out conquering and does indeed conquer—but with a bow, not a sword. That is important, as this signifies long range, first attack conquering, not up close and personal hand-to-hand fighting. Also, the rider *receives* a crown (i.e., does not take one), which means they receive authority.

If you compare this white horse and rider with the one later in Revelation (Rev 19:11–13) you can see that later rider is most definitely Jesus; he has a sword (Word of God) and many crowns. At that later time Jesus comes back to face his enemies, bringing his army clothed in white on white horses too. Again, the notion of white for purity and righteousness is clear.

So, who is the rider on the white horse in Revelation 6:2? You'll find many answers out there, but surely it is the Holy Spirit—a mighty rider conquering many nations and winning many battles over Satan and his powers. The Holy Spirit has spread the gospel message everywhere, with the crown of authority of Jesus as per John 16:7–15, especially verses 13–14:

> When the Spirit of truth comes, he will guide you into all the truth, for he will not speak on his own authority, but whatever he hears he will speak, and he will declare to you the things that are to

Time Block 2A

come. He will glorify me, for he will take what is mine and declare it to you. ᴱˢⱽ

Ultimately, he will conquer. *Anyone* who has the Holy Spirit in them has already conquered Satan and Death, and cannot be beaten by them. The many victories are not through our own strength but through the Spirit making his home in us. We are victorious because the Spirit is victorious.

The Second Seal

A Bright Red Horse with a rider given a mighty sword, and authority to take peace away from the Earth. There will be war and slaughter.

Jesus warns his disciples in Luke 21:9-10 about this particular signifier of the End Times, which is clearly widespread fighting—either civil wars or nation against nation. There can be no argument that this has happened already, at least twice in the twentieth century with the biblical scale of war and slaughter everywhere; not to mention all the wars beforehand, and that have followed. So, without doubt, this second Horse has already come forth and peace on Earth has disappeared.

The following two seals and Horses come later in the timeline, so we will return to those in Time Block 2B on page 28.

Destruction of the Temple

Here is another portion of the Parable of the Wedding Feast in Matthew 22:7. This is when the King destroys the murderers' city.

AD 70 is a well-documented point in time, with a rich written history thanks to the Romans and Jewish historians that recorded what the Romans did (esp. Flavius Josephus)[1], and what happened in Jerusalem. It was not pretty. The Romans sacked Jerusalem after a horrendous siege, destroyed the temple in violent lust and then took the burnt temple apart completely, piece by piece, so not one stone was standing on the other.

This act fulfilled prophecies, mentioned in the New Testament, spoken by Jesus himself in Mark 13:1-2 to his disciples:

> As Jesus was leaving the Temple that day, one of his disciples said, "Teacher, look at these magnificent buildings! Look at the impressive stones in the walls."

---

1. Flavius Josephus, *Of the War - Book VII, Chapter 1*

> Jesus replied, "Yes, look at these great buildings. But they will be completely demolished. Not one stone will be left on top of another!" ᴺᴸᵀ

First Angel of Revelation 14

In Revelation 14, quite a way into the action, three angels fly about declaring individual messages to the bedraggled peoples left at the end, in a sort of summary. However, these three angels' messages can also apply throughout various end-time periods. Here we meet the first one in Revelation 14:6–7:

> And I saw another angel flying through the sky, carrying the eternal Good News to proclaim to the people who belong to this world—to every nation, tribe, language, and people. "Fear God," he shouted. "Give glory to him. For the time has come when he will sit as judge. Worship him who made the heavens, the earth, the sea, and all the springs of water." ᴺᴸᵀ

Do you recognize something from the first sentence? It is the Good News our modern churches proclaim today, to everyone around the world, in so many languages.

The latter part seems easy to scoff at—"for the time has come." People have been ready for this time for centuries, and so modern-day people can look back and say, "Well, Jesus did not come back, so perhaps the church and Bible are wrong? Jesus is never coming back." See the following Bible passage of 2 Peter 3:3–4 as an inspired passage that deals with these thoughts:

> Most importantly, I want to remind you that in the last days scoffers will come, mocking the truth and following their own desires. They will say, "What happened to the promise that Jesus is coming again? From before the times of our ancestors, everything has remained the same since the world was first created." ᴺᴸᵀ

The issue here is the period of time we have lived in (from when Jesus went back to his Father's house to when Groom Jesus is revealed later) is a long, long time for us simple humans—but not for the Father who is being patient. Remember, it is a *necessarily* long time as mentioned before, for the salvation of as many people as possible.

In conclusion, this message from the first angel can fit into Time Blocks 2A, 2B and 3A right before the destruction begins, as that is the message befitting those Time Blocks. It is a huge breath in, held by God, poised, ready for action.

As per typical prophecy, this message from the first angel will also be relevant in the time of the 4th Beast Kingdom coming up later in Time Blocks 4C–4E.

Timeline Segment Summary: Time Block 2A

The following passages for your voluntary deeper study show the Bible verses that speak of the outpouring of God's Holy Spirit to the masses; which was unheard of prior to Jesus's sacrifice and resurrection.

We also have the destruction of the Jewish temple in Jerusalem (second temple) at the hands of the Roman Empire, and the beginnings of Christian persecution that continues to this day.

* Christ Risen eternally: Revelation 5:6–14
* The Holy Spirit comes: Acts 2:1–41, John 14:16–17, 26, John 15:26, John 16:7–15, Joel 2:28–29, Revelation 6:1–2
* Parable of the Wedding Feast continues: Matthew 22:7
* Destruction of the Temple: Luke 19:41–44, Luke 21:20–24, Mark 13:1–2
* Peace taken from the Earth: Mark 13:5–8, Revelation 6:3–4
* The Good News spread across the Earth: Isaiah 12:4–5
* The beginning of Christian persecution: Luke 21:12–19

Time Block 2B

The Formation of Today's Modern World: Revelation 2, Revelation 3, Revelation 6:5–11

The Time Block Overview														
The End Begins	Rise of the Modern World		Jesus Revealed [Day of the LORD]		The Three Terrors					Jesus Returns [Day of the LORD]		1 000-Year Reign		Judgment [Day of the LORD] and New Creation
1	2		3		4					5		6		7
A	A	B	A	B	A	B	C	D	E	A	B	A	B	A	B

The Growth of Today's Societies.
ADxxxx? Modern Times Begin.

The Four Horsemen: Part Two

God tells us we cannot know when Jesus will return, same as the Groom never told the Bride in a Jewish wedding when he'd be back. It was, and will be, a surprise. However, we can know what life will be like around that time, and the flavor of the world at the dawning of his return.

As we saw previously, the infamous Four Horsemen of the Apocalypse present a build-up of the state of the world order beforehand and are well studied. We have already looked at the first two—now to discuss those that are more towards the end of our modern age, due to their non-localized nature.

Time Block 2B

The Third Seal

A Black Horse with rider and weighing scales.

This signifies a great issue with food supply and causes basic food (grains) to cost a day's wage. Luxuries are not touched and are seemingly readily available (note: in John's day, oil and wine are luxuries—see also Proverbs 21:17 in a number of translations).

The size of this scarcity is not revealed; my own thoughts have always assumed it is worldwide, but the Bible does not specifically state that. However, each of the horses is a significant sign, so it is unlikely to be a small local affair; rather, something anyone reading the Bible could see and agree on.

This brings me to why this third horse is more a global effect in this modern time of Time Block 2B, rather than before: as farming now has to produce food for almost eight times more people than in 1800. This food then has to be distributed through a complex supply chain, which in 2022 began to prove unreliable through unforeseen circumstances.

The manufacture of luxuries just requires a workforce and raw materials which are, for the most part, readily available through mining.

Therefore, so long as there is a market for luxuries, and a workforce that can mine the materials and create them (even a robotic workforce), there's no end to the *manufactured* goods we can make; but food is at risk as we have to grow and sustain crops through water, land, energy costs and management. You can't mine potatoes or grains.

We now rely on industrial agriculture to produce most of our food, but arable land is not increasing. Add the cost and amount of energy needed to do industrial agriculture, and it shows that this food risk is only going to increase as our world population continues to increase and arable land continues its decline. Throw in an unexpected war in Europe (Russia invaded Ukraine) which affects one of the major grain producers of the Western world, and you begin to see what a rickety system we all rely on.

Therefore, since the late 1800s, we have built the complex infrastructure, reliance, massive population explosion and means to produce the Black Horse and Rider on a global scale.

The Fourth Seal

A Pale Horse with Death as its rider and The Grave following.

These two symbolic creatures kill one-fourth of the earth's population with sword (which is war and fighting), famine, pestilence (which is disease), and importantly wild animals or beasts.

Like the second Red Horse described as affecting the earth, this Horse and Rider is undeniably global in scale as John describes seeing a fourth of the earth's population killed. Currently that is approximately two billion people, which we haven't seen yet; but the similarity of events building in the twenty-first century cannot be ignored.

The Four Horses—A Conclusion to be Drawn

Revelation 6:1–9 is similar to a lot of world history, with the spread of the Bible, the countless wars, hyper-inflation, famine, and disease widespread. The twentieth century was an almost endless example of these horses somewhere on the Earth. Indeed, the Typical Prophecy style society written about in the future in Habakkuk 2:2–19 could also align with the building of the modern world c. AD 1800 to 1900, as well as the Israelites of the time of writing, and the society at the end of the Beast Kingdom in Time Block 4E to come. Take a pause and go and read that scripture and you will surely see the repeated pattern of power, corruption, greed, and lack of care that humanity seems drawn to.

So, if Revelation 6:1-9 is so similar to what we've experienced globally already, how can we know how close we are to the revealing of Christ? What is the one thing that stands out as *not* fulfilled?

Here is an important sanity check from Revelation 6:8:

> . . . These two were given authority over one-fourth of the earth, to kill with the sword and famine and disease and wild animals.[NLT]

In the history of mankind, there has never been *widespread* death by wild animals or beasts in the scale mentioned.

Most of what the four horses and riders do could relate to a lot of history, as mentioned above—the Christian Reformation, the First and Second World Wars, Great Depression, Smallpox, and Spanish Flu of the 1920s and '30s are very relatable. The Black Death that ravaged Europe in the 1300s is another case for the Pale Horse. Yet, that one mention of the death by wild animals or beasts (not parasites carried by mosquitoes or other insects, but "beasts" in context with what John knew) is a signpost we cannot ignore. This helps us understand where we are in the timeline.

To check, here are some simple mathematics: at the time of writing, there are approximately eight billion people on Earth. One-fourth of this would be two billion people killed by war, famine, disease, and beasts. If we assume an even split for simplicity, that would be beasts killing *500 million people!*

Now, nowhere in the verse of Revelation 6:8 does it say it is an even split, so how small a proportion should it be? Surely a significant number or else Jesus would not have shown John that beasts are involved at the end. When I wrote this, we were nowhere near 100 million people killed directly by wild beasts—not even 50 million. Depending on the source, most are killed by dogs or snakes and the numbers vary between 100,000 and 20,000 people.[1] There can be no denying that we are yet to reach the point in Revelation where the Pale Horse, Death, and the Grave come to the culmination of their work through wild beasts.

As for pestilence, COVID 19 as of April 13th, 2024, reportedly killed approximately 7 million people[2] which again is not reaching the level of Revelation 6:8 yet. However, it does keep mutating and seems to be here to stay. To reach the pestilence levels of the Pale Horse, you would need to see a disease like Smallpox, Ebola, or Bubonic Plague become a pandemic.

So, we are NOT past Revelation 6:8 yet at the time of writing. That is clear. Indeed, looking at those numbers, you can see that something very significant happens to the human race on a massive scale; worse than the wars of the twentieth century and COVID 19 of the twenty-first century. We can therefore conclude that at this time of writing, the Black Horse is getting ready, and the Pale Horse is to come.

ADxxxx? When do Modern Times Begin?

The blurring between Time Block 2A and Time Block 2B makes it hard to say when exactly we entered the final Modern age. Is it the rise of science?

---

1. https://en.wikipedia.org/wiki/List_of_deadliest_animals_to_humans (note: mosquitoes do not kill humans, but rather the parasites they carry do – so, this would come under 'pestilence')

2. According to World-o-Meter website: https://www.worldometers.info/coronavirus/coronavirus-death-toll/ for that date.

The Industrial Revolution of Europe? The global empire of the British in the 1800s? Is it the invention of the transistor and then computers? Or the internet and social media?

I believe it is around 1980, but I have to stress that this is *my personal idea and not from the Holy Spirit*. Perhaps other times in history will speak to you personally as to when modern times began.

My personal viewpoint as to why 1980 was the start of Time Block 2B rests with mass social interconnectivity and lack of control over material. I believe this coming together of home computing and the internet connectivity is the start of Time Block 2B; ending in a self-centered, self-absorbed, and self-focused society where the individual gains are the drives, as the Bible tells us in 2 Timothy 3:1–5:

> You should know this, Timothy, that in the last days there will be very difficult times. For people will love only themselves and their money. They will be boastful and proud, scoffing at God, disobedient to their parents, and ungrateful. They will consider nothing sacred. They will be unloving and unforgiving; they will slander others and have no self-control. They will be cruel and hate what is good. They will betray their friends, be reckless, be puffed up with pride, and love pleasure rather than God. They will act religious, but they will reject the power that could make them godly. Stay away from people like that!^{NLT}

It all has to do with freedom to see, read, and write anything that is truth, mistruth, lies, as well as being able to freely present, or see, mentally damaging imagery and viewpoints. This has always been a difficult question with society—is censorship and moral leadership needed? Or should the censorship and morality rest solely on the individual? Control vs Freedom?

From a Biblical standpoint, God has always set boundaries for how we are to act with ourselves and with others—the Ten Commandments are a well-known example. Total freedom to do whatever you wish is not part of God's plan for us. Why? Perhaps due to the nature of our curiosity and willingness to experiment and try *anything*, and to also to create seemingly whole truths from a grain of fact that fits what we wish.

Enter the internet skeleton and the World Wide Web skin; both powerful tools handed out to provide great freedom. Today the internet has spread almost across the entire world—and this has become a two-edged sword for great good and for great bad.

Time Block 2B

For good—people in desperate trouble can show live streams of their suffering to achieve global support and affect change for great good. But others can generate endless conspiracy theory half-truths and misinformation that derails a society. We have had propaganda and misinformation eating away at humanity for a long, long time—but now it spreads at a phenomenal rate.

Families and friends can connect across great distances and communicate like never before. Yet social media can be used as a psychological tool to destroy an individual, no matter how far away they are.

Then there is imagery: We can send and share all kinds of beautiful pictures and photos to the world—but pornography and violence of all flavors and its degrading nature are available to all members of a family who have a device connected to an internet server.

Would you feel happy to leave young children and newly forming adults with this uncaring and unchecked entity for hours? To learn social skills, self-censorship, sexual education and to absorb unfettered viewpoints, half-truth propaganda? The uncomfortable truth is, we do.

In conclusion, I chose 1980 as what I believe to be the starting point of a growing mindset no longer trained by community cultural social responsibilities, or held back by some negative feedback to rein in extremes. In a way, we now have formative education via an anti-moral anarchy. This society is alluded to in the Bible passages shown in Time Block 2B; it is forming through the mechanism of (interestingly) complete freedom to express, be, or do anything.

How Long Have We Got? Give a Date!

This modern age will continue for as long as the Father wills it, and then the end will come with the revealing of Jesus as seen in the upcoming Time Block 3A. No one knows this date, *not even Jesus*. He tells us this in the Bible, see Mark 13:32–37. Here are verses 32–33:

> "However, no one knows the day or hour when these things will happen, not even the angels in heaven or the Son himself. Only the Father knows. And since you don't know when that time will come, be on guard! Stay alert!" NLT

He also clearly points to the fact it will be incredibly sudden, so much so that no one will really have any chance to stand there and say, "Oh look,

I think Jesus might be coming back." That sentence, in itself, is probably too long to say for the time it takes Jesus to be revealed.

Note something very important: Jesus will only come back at the command of the Father part of God, as per the requirements of the Jewish Wedding! This means, and Jesus admitted it, that the Human aspect of God does not know when the Father aspect of God is going to do this. It also means that no mere human or any angel/demon can tell you when Jesus is going to return.

If anyone—no matter how clever, famous, or followed by millions on social media, convincingly explains mysterious signs, performs many calculations—tells you a date for when the Groom Jesus is returning to get his Bride—*they are mistaken, or worse, lying.*

Let me just repeat that: If a human sets a date for Jesus's return, they are wrong. That simple. Indeed, even if a bright and glorious angel gives a date, he is lying. You hear a voice from heaven? Choosing you to know, right? No, you are mistaken. Why would God tell any of us and not Jesus? Who is more important? Never forget that truth, for this delusion of "knowing the date" has affected many fervently religious people.

The Wedding Feast Parable Continues

In this Time Block, we have another section of the wedding parable applied to the timeline in Matthew 22:8–9. Here, the king declares the original invitees to be no longer worthy because they ignored him and did nasty things to his messengers. So, instead, he now sends out the invite for his superb feast to anyone they can find. This is the invite taken by the Apostles to the world, through the work of the Holy Spirit.

Did you catch that? The King has invited the *whole world* to join him in the feast. See those Bibles? They are everywhere and the perfect invite. Bibles didn't exist in or before Jesus's time. The Israelis had scriptures on scrolls, but not assembled into one easy reference book. The apostles, the churches, various crucial people throughout our turbulent end-time history have been going to everywhere they can, inviting all they can find. *Right now* is your chance to accept that invitation and come to the feast too! Remember—the first angel of Revelation 14 says it. This time does not last forever.

Time Block 2B

What Sort of People Will Dominate the World?

Ah, that's easy. As we have seen before on page 32, Paul warned Timothy about these in 2 Timothy 3:1–5.

These people will be widespread, and don't we already take this sort of behavior for granted? I am a Christian and guilty of many of those traits myself; who isn't? But these people are super-liberal/conservative, super-entitled, super self-serving. Everything is allowable for self-justification, self-fulfillment, and self-entitlement.

Self is the dominating mindset which is the exact opposite of God's.

All that matters is who one is and what one can get for oneself in pleasure, money, sex, power, occult, and violence. Extreme conservatism is the opposite to some of the traits these people will have, but again, extreme conservatism will also produce many of these traits. Let's face facts: any extreme tends to be bad. Although Jesus declares he "spits out" tepid, lukewarm works in Revelation 3:15–17 we must not read this to mean we need to hit the extreme end-stops of any opinion, work, or politics. You can be Hot. You can be Cold. But to be Scalding or Freezing is clearly too far and damaging.

So, if you reach a point where traits of narcissism and comfortable religion dominate world societies, you will know time is short. As I am writing this I can see these sorts of societies clearly forming but we are not engulfed in this sort of behavior yet. As far as I know, we have time, but be awake to what is happening.

Note that wisdom has something to say, out loud: Proverbs 1:20–23:

> Wisdom cries aloud in the street, in the markets she raises her voice; at the head of the noisy streets she cries out; at the entrance of the city gates she speaks: "How long, O simple ones, will you love being simple? How long will scoffers delight in their scoffing and fools hate knowledge?"
>
> If you turn at my reproof, behold, I will pour out my spirit to you; I will make my words known to you. ᴱˢⱽ

Wisdom calls out to these people as much as possible. Do they listen?

Isaiah prophesied about our modern times, with empty religion driven by mankind and people rejecting the God that made them. However, Isaiah recorded that there are deaf people hearing the words of a book, and out of the gloom and the darkness the eyes of the blind shall see. This is both a clear reference to Jesus reading from scripture in his day and the healing he performed, coupled with a nod to the Bible and its results in the period of time it has existed (Time Block 2A and 2B).

And finally, look at a society God does not approve of—Isaiah 2:6–8. This could so easily relate to all the wealth, vehicles, and cherished objects we have here in the West:

> For the Lord has rejected his people, the descendants of Jacob, because they have filled their land with practices from the East and with sorcerers, as the Philistines do. They have made alliances with pagans. Israel is full of silver and gold; there is no end to its treasures. Their land is full of warhorses; there is no end to its chariots. Their land is full of idols; the people worship things they have made with their own hands. ᴺᴸᵀ

A Comment About Luke 21:7–36

For a relevant look at Jesus talking about the end times to come after his ministry, take the time for a thoughtful read of Luke 21:7–36. These verses, spoken by Jesus, contain a lot of prophecy. Remember I said that the Bible can use repetition, jump about in time and verses may be applied to more than one event? Luke 21:7–36 is indeed a portion of the Bible that does just this.

Here is my understanding of what is happening:

1. Jesus prophesied the destruction of the Temple in AD 70 here, clearly. See Time Block 2A previously in this guide; this is Luke 21:8–24, especially Luke 21:20–2. If you read the actual history of what went on with the Roman siege of Jerusalem, you'd say "yes, clearly."

2. But Luke 21:8–11 *also* relates well with the time before the revelation of Christ in Time Block 3A to come, and the destruction wrought in Time Block 3B; as does Luke 21:25–26.

3. Immediately, Jesus states that the Day of the Lord will occur after that: "Then they will see the Son of Man coming in a cloud with great power and glory" which can be both the first Day of the Lord (the revealing) in Time Block 3A, and the second Day of the Lord (the return) in Time Block 5A. In both cases, it is the time for any follower of Christ to be saved from the coming immense horror.

4. Luke 21:28–31 is for the Modern Times, Time Block 2B. It is a warning to be aware.

5. Then it would seem the words spoken in Luke 21:32–35 cover the destruction of the current world order by the "Terrors," with Luke 21:34–35 being especially about Time Block 3A (the sudden and unexpected return).

6. And finally, Luke 21:36 is a comment aimed at the entire end times, from 2B to 7A when we have the chance to escape the coming horrors through prayer and alertness.

So, you can see Jesus seems not to speak linearly. He repeated ideas to show milestones and covered small time periods and vast ones in one sermon.

Timeline Segment Summary: Time Block 2B

The following study points have a lot of Bible verses to look at because, interestingly, there is so much prophecy and scripture about our period of mankind's history! It is a very important time as Jesus warns us to be awake to the signs and be ready.

* What society and people will be like right before Jesus returns: Isaiah 2:7–8, Isaiah 29:13–21, Habakkuk 2:2–19, 2 Timothy 3:1–5, 2 Timothy 4:3–4, 2 Peter 2:1–22, 1 John 2:15–17, Jude 4–19 and Revelation 3:15–22
* The spread of the gospel and Bible across the world: Isaiah 12:3–5
* The Parable of the Wedding Feast continues: Matthew 22:8–9
* So, where is Jesus? Habakkuk 2:2–3, 2 Peter 3:1–9, Revelation 3:10–11
* Christian Persecution continues today and to the end: Luke 21:12–19, Revelation 6:9–11
* The warning signs of widespread inflation, war, disease, famine, and odd significant attacks by wild animals: Deuteronomy 32:22–24, Luke 21:9–11, Revelation 6:5–8
* Pay attention: Isaiah 28:7–29, Proverbs 1:20–33, Zephaniah 2:1–3, Mark 4:24–25, Luke 21:28–31, Revelation 3:1–6, Revelation 14:6–7
* The end of this Age begins suddenly: Luke 21:25–28

Interlude

Important Points About the Sun, Moon, and Stars

In the upcoming Time Block 3A, we will see an allotted time signified by two simultaneous portents: one is a blood-red full moon, the other is a black sun. However, a problem with studying the end times is another event declared as the Day of the Lord, which has a darkened sun. This is near the end.

There are many examples of the wrath of God named the Day of the Lord. The same type of day is mentioned—a day with darkness, gloom, darkened sun, darkened moon, and stars falling or not giving any light. However, there is *one* very special Day of the Lord set apart from all the others. The Red Moon and Black Sun. Everything else matches the typical prophecy, with the *exception* of the color of the moon. So, why does it matter?

It is all about the certainty of *when*. Only God the Father knows the timing of one of the events. Jesus tells us that even he doesn't know, if you recall my spiel on page 33 guarding you against anyone or anything that tells you when Jesus is to return.

However, the timing of one of the Day of the Lord days does have a distinct timeframe; given by Daniel and clearly alluded to by Jesus in Matthew 24:15. It is 1 290 days after the False Prophet (also known as The Antichrist) erects the statue to the Beast King and declares it god (Daniel 12:11). This is ok, because we don't know exactly when the False Prophet will do this erecting; but when it does happen, we can start the clock and wait for the Day of the Lord and the physical return of Jesus to reign on Earth for 1 000-years.

With this in mind, it is important to understand the Red Moon event is not the same time period as the second Day of the Lord event. Instead, a

INTERLUDE

dark moon, darkened sun, will signify the second one. See the difference? On that Time Block 5A Day of The Lord there will be no light shining at all, and yet it will be like day.

For the event that has the red moon and black sun, you should also consider that it cannot be an eclipse of the sun, because during the Biblical event, the sun looks black as sackcloth and the moon red as blood. This means both are visible at the same time. I have seen two solar eclipses now, thanks to God's grace, and I can tell you the moon does not look crimson like blood when the sun is behind it. It looks black. And guess what—you can't see the sun! For the black sun and red moon to be seen together, something else blocks out the sun's light. Perhaps God's will alone?

Another rather important point to consider is that Jesus returns (the first "second coming") and is *revealed* at the Red Moon/Black Sun event and does not touch down on the Earth. This is the "Revelation of Jesus Christ," as mentioned in 1 Peter 1:13, also as described in the first sentence of the Book of Revelation. Some Bible translations say "Revelation *from* Jesus Christ." However, as Peter tells us to be ready for the revelation *of* Jesus Christ (or when Jesus Christ is revealed as per the New Living Translation), the Book of Revelation is about the world being shown the Groom as the Groom is revealed to the world and everything that occurs because of this.

Jesus certainly does return once more with his army of Angels and Saints in the darkened sun/dark moon event; that is his physical Second Coming, to remain *on* Earth and rule for 1 000-years.

For those who wish to dig deeper, on the follow pages are tables of the typical Day of The Lord prophecies including the Red Moon special case. I have also presented what is to happen before, after, and during to show that I have hopefully listened to the Holy Spirit correctly.

	Black Sun, Red Moon	
	Joel 2:28–32	Revelation 6:1–16
Before	Holy Spirit is poured out on all Mankind.	The Four Horsemen, culminating in a fourth of the Earth killed by sword, famine, pestilence, and wild beasts.
During	There will be wonders in the heavens and on the earth, blood and fire, and columns of smoke. The sun shall be turned to darkness, and the moon to blood, before the great and awesome day of the Lord comes.	A great earthquake, and the sun became black as sackcloth, the full moon became like blood. Stars fall to the Earth like figs from a tree. Sky split apart (rolled up like a scroll) and every mountain and island moved from its place.
After	Everyone who calls on the name of the Lord shall be saved. In Mount Zion and Jerusalem there shall be those who escape, as the Lord has said, and among the survivors shall be those whom the Lord calls.	Everyone hides from the presence of God and the wrath of the Lamb. (See also Isaiah 2:9–10,17–19)

Interlude

			Darkened Sun, Dark Moon	
	Joel 2:1–14	Joel 3:9–21	Mark 13:14–27, Matthew 24:15–31	Zechariah 14:6–7
Before	A massive army is coming.	Nations gather against Israel. Time to harvest the grapes.	The Abomination of Desolation set up. Great tribulation the like of which has not occurred since the beginning of time. Many false Christs and False Prophets.	The Lord will fight the nations. The Mount of Olives will split apart.
During	Earthquakes and trembling heavens. The sun and moon grow dark, and the stars no longer shine. The Day of the Lord is indeed great and very awesome.	The sun and moon will grow dark, and the stars will no longer shine. Heavens and Earth tremble.	The sun will be darkened, the moon will give no light, the stars will fall from the sky, and the powers in the heavens will be shaken. Jesus comes with great power and glory, and gathers the elect from the farthest corners of Heaven and Earth.	The sources of light will no longer shine, yet there will be daylight. No normal day and night, for at evening it will still be light.
After	The Lord says to return to him, with all your heart, with fasting weeping and mourning.	God dwells on Earth. Mountains drip with sweet wine and the hills flow with milk. A spring will flow out from Temple		And the Lord will be king over all the earth. There will be one Lord—his name alone will be worshipped.

Time Block 3A

Jesus is Revealed—the Day of the Lord: Revelation 6:12–17, Revelation 7

The Time Block Overview							
The End Begins	Rise of the Modern World	Jesus Revealed [Day of the LORD]	The Three Terrors			Jesus Returns [Day of the LORD]	1 000-Year Reign	Judgment [Day of the LORD] and New Creation
1	2	3	4			5	6	7
A	A | B	A | B	A | B | C | D | E			A | B	A | B	A | B

The Return of the Groom for the Bride.
The Revelation of Jesus!

Warning! A Second Coming of Christ

This Revealing of Christ is a major event in all the end times. It is the dividing line between the increasing birth pains of the new creation at the end of Time Block 2B, and the total finish of our modern world. Christ's revealing is the kick-off to a lot of destruction, unholy creatures, amazing celestial events, a major rebirth of a New World Order, and a special king under the power of Satan.

As mentioned previously, the Revealing of Christ is not the same 2nd Coming of Christ as per Time Block 5A, where Jesus comes back to stay for

Time Block 3A

1 000 years, as can be seen in the chapter heading table. Confused? You are not alone.

Now, Jesus returns on the clouds of Heaven but *without his Angels or Saints*; he is somehow revealed to all the world at once as per Revelation 1:7:

> Look! He comes with the clouds of heaven. And everyone will see him—even those who pierced him. And all the nations of the world will mourn for him. Yes! Amen! NLT

Also we have Peter's warnings to be prepared for action and sober minded in 1 Peter 1:13:

> So prepare your minds for action and exercise self-control. Put all your hope in the gracious salvation that will come to you when Jesus Christ is revealed to the world. NLT

Why does Jesus do this? What is the point of turning up and not staying or touching down on Earth this time? When I was a young lad, I thought the first we see of God would be a Judgment Day I had heard about—where the world is destroyed and we all face God in Heaven as he sits on a Throne; but wait, that's not what the Bible says.

Remember the Jewish Wedding? Well, before the merriment and Heaven part, the Groom has to come back and take his bride away to complete the *start* of the ceremony. Here, with the Black Sun/Red Moon event we see this very return of the Groom, at his Father's command, to gather his Bride. Remember who the Bride is? See page 15 if you need a reminder.

Recall the first steps in a Hebrew wedding: the Bride and Groom are contractually married and considered one, but this is not the complete ceremony. The Groom goes away for a time (potentially a year)[1] before returning to gather up his Bride for the next part of the wedding.

Often the groom would come back unexpectedly towards the end of the period away, and the Bride had to be ready, knowing that her Groom was returning as promised. Jesus told a parable of the wise and foolish bridesmaids (Matthew 25:1–13), to show there would be a time to address short-comings if you are wise and understand the nature of the sudden return.

---

1. Glenn Kay, Jewish Wedding Customs and the Bride of Messiah

Also, in 1 Thessalonians 5:1–11, Paul tells us that people will say "everything is peaceful and secure" before disaster falls upon them. Here are verses 1–3:

> Now concerning the times and the seasons, brothers, you have no need to have anything written to you. For you yourselves are fully aware that the Day of the Lord will come like a thief in the night. While people are saying, "There is peace and security," then sudden destruction will come upon them as labor pains come upon a pregnant woman, and they will not escape. ESV

This return of Jesus that Paul talks about cannot be the other return in Time Block 5A, due to what is going on before that particular Time Block—in that there is a massive battle with the Beast Kingdom. Hardly comfort and peace!

Whereas today, in most of the Western world (Time Block 2B), we have had relative peace, comfort and security for quite a while.

Therefore, somewhere between the people declaring "everything is peaceful and secure" near the end of Time Block 2B, and Jesus's return in Time Block 3A, we must squeeze in Revelation 6:7–8 quite suddenly:

> When the Lamb broke the fourth seal, I heard the fourth living being say, "Come!" I looked up and saw a horse whose color was pale green. Its rider was named Death, and his companion was the Grave. These two were given authority over one-fourth of the earth, to kill with the sword and famine and disease and wild animals. NLT

This shows that whatever happens to the Modern World comes on quickly, as if someone has flicked a switch and thrown everyone into turmoil. Then during this turmoil, Jesus is revealed quickly (i.e., suddenly, unexpectedly).

The Elect

During this Time Block, before great destruction begins, an elect group of Israelites are introduced: 12 000 are marked from each of the ancient tribes for God as bondservants, totaling 144 000 (Revelation 7:3–8). When I was a child, I thought that these were the sum total of all those saved, but that's not what God says. These chosen are not from the Christian church or any such followers and acceptors of the Grace of God through Jesus;

Time Block 3A

but specifically 144,000 *Israelites*. We know this because immediately after they are sealed we are shown the Multitude from every nation crying out 'Salvation belongs to our God who sits on the throne, and to the Lamb!'"[ESV] Clearly the multitude are the church, or Bride of the Lamb of God, namely Christians.

This selection of the Elect is important as these 144 000 remain on the Earth through the coming destruction and Beast Kingdom, and are a special offering to the Lord as we will see later.

So what happens to the rest of the Israelites? The Apostle Paul deals with this in Romans 11. Firstly, he puts forth the idea of a special remnant set aside, illustrating the past and linking it to the future. See Romans 11:5–7:

> So too at the present time there is a remnant, chosen by grace. But if it is by grace, it is no longer on the basis of works; otherwise grace would no longer be grace.
> What then? Israel failed to obtain what it was seeking. The elect obtained it, but the rest were hardened . . . [ESV]

Paul then goes on to tell us what happens to the rest of the Israelites that are not the remnant (144 000), in Romans 11:25–27:

> I want you to understand this mystery, dear brothers and sisters, so that you will not feel proud about yourselves. Some of the people of Israel have hard hearts, but this will last only until the full number of Gentiles comes to Christ. And so all Israel will be saved. As the Scriptures say,
> "The one who rescues will come from Jerusalem,
>   and he will turn Israel away from ungodliness.
> And this is my covenant with them,
>   that I will take away their sins."[NLT]

Therefore, at some point in the future (Time Block 5A, 5B and 6A when the Deliverer, Jesus the Messiah, returns), all Israel come to accept Jesus as Lord and are saved, seemingly through the fullness of the grace given to the Gentiles (the rest of us), and the mercy of God to take away the sins of the Israelites by his action, not theirs.

Let's Talk About Rapture

This is a very hot topic of the church, especially as we race towards the Revealing of Christ and a lot of hope from Christians that we will be removed before anything bad happens. This is a confused topic, emotionally charged and divisive even with the base truths spoken by both Jesus and the Apostles. So many settled beliefs surround Rapture that you will get camps of Christians that are "Pre-Tribulation," "Mid-Tribulation," and "Post-Tribulation" believers, and perhaps even those that don't think any Rapture will happen at all.

Indeed, after many passes through this subject writing this section, the Holy Spirit warned me I had not got it right myself—that I had discerned wrongly. Therefore, I have re-written this as a more open section. It is better to present you with the Bible verses and truths, and let you make up your own mind through prayer to God and meditation on his answer, than for me to willingly be a false teacher leading you astray.

Firstly, if you are looking for a distinct time for the Rapture event, where everyone who is a follower of Christ is taken up into the air in an instant to be with him, then I suggest you may have trouble. Do not get my intentions wrong; there's plenty of evidence for a removal of saints, martyrs, and even the Bride, but being very specific in timing is going to cause you more harm than good. Why? Let's rewind history and show you what can happen when believers get fixated.

What did the people of Jerusalem say to Jesus in John 12:33–34? They were confused because they were certain that Christ was staying as the Eternal King, so they made up their minds that God Incarnate there before them was wrong and could not be the King of Kings they expected, so who was he? There are more examples I found in the gospel of John that reinforces this idea that people knew their scripture very well, just not the time they were in; see also John 7:25–27:

> *Can This Be the Christ?*
>
> Some of the people of Jerusalem therefore said, "Is not this the man whom they seek to kill? And here he is, speaking openly, and they say nothing to him! Can it be that the authorities really know that this is the Christ? But we know where this man comes from, and when the Christ appears, no one will know where he comes from." ESV

Time Block 3A

If you excuse the odd tense; the truth was, he is The Christ (The Messiah), and will be ruling from Earth, but not when they thought. Other events had to happen, and still *have* to happen, and Jesus told his disciples and anyone who wanted to listen, that this was the case.

Now, back to Rapture: there are obvious passages and scripture that back up the spectacular removal and transformation of some of the dead and living servants of the Lord Jesus; but when and how is a little foggy and full of confusion and argument. Remember, the Holy Spirit is *not* a Spirit of confusion, as he speaks only what he hears from Christ (John 16:13-15). So, who is the spirit of deception and confusion that is attacking the church and splitting them asunder?

Think on this: the Word of God declares that you may be kept from the hour of tribulation that comes upon the earth (Revelation 3:10), and to rest as the fury passes (Isaiah 26:19-21). However, the Word of God also says this is the case if you give up your life (Luke 17:30-33) and if you have endured, are ready, prepared, and strong in character to escape the day and stand before Jesus (Revelation 7:9-17).

So what is more important? Knowing *when* and perhaps becoming obsessed like the people who missed who Jesus was in Jerusalem over 2 000 years ago? Or, attempting to be a complete and prepared follower of Christ, as Jesus warns us in Luke 21:34-36:

> "Watch out! Don't let your hearts be dulled by carousing and drunkenness, and by the worries of this life. Don't let that day catch you unaware, like a trap. For that day will come upon everyone living on the earth. Keep alert at all times. And pray that you might be strong enough to escape these coming horrors and stand before the Son of Man." NLT

God's will be done when he says so.

Here are some themes you should look at and understand:

Be Ready!

As you have just read, from the mouth of God—Jesus tells us to keep alert at all times, don't be dulled with carousing, drunkenness, and worries of this life. He also strongly warns a church in Revelation 3:1-3 to wake up or he will turn up unexpectedly against them. The Bride must be ceremonially washed, clean, and waiting for her Groom who comes unannounced to bring her back to his Father's house. Servants must be acting as if they are ready for their master's return, or face punishment (see Matthew 24:42-51, Luke 12:35-48).

Peter also warns us in 1 Peter 1:13-19 to be holy as he (God) is holy and not to conform to passions of your past life; and Paul gives good advice in 1 Thessalonians 5:1-11, 23-24 where again the notion is to be awake and clear-headed. He also says be protected by the armor of faith and love, and put on the helmet of confidence in salvation.

Psalm 15 helps you understand the sort of person that will stand firm, and not be shaken. Although David was speaking about a temple and entering into the Lord's presence, God has not changed. What was required then to be in the presence of God, is required now.

Therefore, rapture conclusion number one is clear: be prepared, be ready, and be fitting to be taken by your Groom—the Lamb of God, Jesus. What happens if you are a Christian, but are not ready? That is an important point to ponder. You are saved, but are you raptured?

If You Lose Your Life, You Will Keep It

When you read what Jesus tells us in Luke 17:22-37 you get an interesting fact. He starts with telling the disciples they will not see the days of the Son of Man, and then goes on to describe what society will be like before the sudden and unexpected return of the Son of Man on his day. It will be business as usual. However, the crucial thing to remember is: when Jesus returns to the whole world unexpectedly and suddenly, if you try to *preserve* or keep your life, like Lot's wife, you will lose it. And if you lose your life, you will keep it.

One person will be taken, the other will not. Both are in the same place, doing the same thing.

It seems to me (and let me state this is *my personal opinion*), that when the Son of Man is revealed to the whole world, if we try to stay and go back to everything we have (wife, husband, family, friends, children, pets, house, car, valuables) we will lose our life. And if we stand, look up, greet Jesus, and are willing to give up everything (including our life), ready and prepared and joyful to see him (not scared and worried), we keep our life. Read also Hebrews 10:35-39, which in the English Standard Version (and others) it talks about the Lord taking no pleasure in those that shrink back.

Time Block 3A

One way to look at this in context of a Jewish groom coming back to gather up his bride after the time apart—if the groom arrived and his betrothed wife shrank back in fear, horror, or anger at the groom's appearance, what would be the response on a human level? For me, I would wonder if the Bride truly did love me, and really did want to come to her new life.

Therefore, conclusion number two about rapture is mysterious: we are to lose our life suddenly and unexpectedly to keep it. Do not look back like Lot's wife, having a heart settled in this world and reluctantly wondering if you want to go onwards with Jesus to his Father's house.

There Are at Least Three Gatherings

Looking at them in reverse order, distant future to near future: when Jesus is talking in Matthew 24:15–31, he is speaking of the time of return after the Beast Kingdom, when the Elect are gathered. The Elect, as mentioned on page 44, are a special offering to the Lord; they stay on Earth during the Terrors and Jesus gathers them as he returns with all his angels in might and glory, with the trumpet call of Time Block 5A. So, right there you have a specific gathering of 144 000 people.

Prior to this, the saints and martyrs are harvested during the Mighty Battle of Time Block 4E, as per Revelation 14:15–16:

> *The Harvest of the Earth*
> And another angel came out of the temple, calling with a loud voice to him who sat on the cloud, "Put in your sickle, and reap, for the hour to reap has come, for the harvest of the earth is fully ripe." So he who sat on the cloud swung his sickle across the earth, and the earth was reaped. ESV

So that's two gatherings.

Before these two then, in the near future—what of the Bride of Christ? This is the Rapture; before the wrath of God that follows through Time Block 3A and beyond. What does the Bible say here? Revelation 7:9–14 helps us understand what sort of peoples these are.

Here are verses 9, 10, and 14:

> After this I looked, and behold, a great multitude that no one could number, from every nation, from all tribes and peoples and languages, standing before the throne and before the Lamb, clothed in white robes, with palm branches in their hands, and crying out

with a loud voice, "Salvation belongs to our God who sits on the throne, and to the Lamb!"

. . . And he said to me, "These are the ones coming out of the great tribulation. They have washed their robes and made them white in the blood of the Lamb." ESV

These verses strongly suggest "Christians" and it can be noted that they have escaped something bad as it was happening. In some translations of the Bible (for example the New Living Translation), the people are said to have "died" in the great tribulation which would suggest rapture does not happen before tribulation takes the multitude.

However, I believe the English Standard Version is the more accurate, as Jesus told us in John 14:2–3 that he has gone and prepared a place for us and will come and get us and take us to himself. That relates to the Jewish Wedding idea of the Groom coming back to take his Bride back to his father's house, where there was a place made ready for her new life.

As part of the wedding ceremony, the Bride and Groom go to a quiet place for a short while before the rousing wedding feast. There is a short, quiet period for reflection in Revelation 8:1 before the wrath begins in earnest. Be aware though, the wrath is *not* the rousing wedding feast—the feast occurs when Jesus and his Bride return to be shown to the world in Time Block 5A.

If the multitude are the Bride, then what must a Bride do before their Groom comes back unannounced? See the preceding points 1 and 2 above—be prepared, ritually washed (baptized), clean, blameless, leaving/losing past lives, being ready, and worthy. And what about bridesmaids? See Matthew 25:1–13. Again—those that are prepared and ready will go in with the Bride and Groom, but those that are slumbering end up asking to be let in and being told, "I don't know you." The message is clear—*be prepared*!

So, for conclusion number three about rapture: there is more than one gathering. The one coming up first seems to be for the Bride to escape the wrath; but the Bride is a certain sort of prepared and ready Christian.

Other Passages to Consider for Rapture

Now you have some conclusions to mull over and decide, through prayer and meditation on the Word, to see what discernment you have with respect to Rapture. As you do so, remember one VERY important point: the notion of rapture and salvation are two separate things. If rapture is confusing and

Time Block 3A

mysterious, the Lamb's Book of Life is not. I can definitely say that not being raptured (or gathered) *does not exclude you* from the Book of Life! Only the rejection of Jesus will do that.

To help you, here are some other passages to understand:

* Hebrews 9:28 tells us that Christ, being offered once to bear our sins will return again, not to deal with sin, but to save those that eagerly await him

* If you read Luke 21:25–28 Jesus tells us that there will be strange signs in the sun, moon and stars, odd tides, and roaring seas; and when these things *begin* to take place, "stand and look up for your salvation is near." During this passage Jesus states that he will be coming on the clouds of Heaven, which he says in Revelation 1:7–8. In the Revelation passage, Jesus also adds that the Nations will mourn over his return—why?

* Colossians 3:4 tells us when Christ is revealed, the followers of Christ will also be revealed with him in glory. The Revelation of Christ is this Time Block we currently studying (3A)

* Philippians 3:20–21 is more towards Time Block 4E (Great Battle) or 5A (Christ Returns to Rule) due to Paul talking about Jesus bringing everything under his authority, and changing our humble bodies to be like his glorified body (the First Resurrection, Time Block 5B)

* Revelation 7:9–17 shows us a multitude from every nation, declaring that salvation belongs to our God who sits on the Throne (in heaven) and to the Lamb. These serve God in his temple and are the First Resurrection of Revelation 20:6 (as above)

* First Thessalonians 4:15–18 talks about the trump of God and voice of an Archangel. This again is more towards Time Block 4E and 5A, where the taking up of the tribulation saints and the 144 000 occurs. The Thessalonians passage also talks about meeting Jesus in the clouds—which also matches Christ coming on the clouds of Heaven as stated in Matthew 26:64 and Mark 14:62 (where Jesus declares I AM in context that he is the Messiah), and told to us in Daniel 7:13

Finally, as we leave Rapture and move on, there is an important point to think about humbly: the time right *before* the Black Sun/Red Moon is not a peachy time for anyone; Israelite, Christian, Buddhist, Muslim, etc., as reading Revelations 6:4–9 will tell you. Before, during, or after this bridal rapture there will be widespread horrible war, death, famine, and pestilence. So, if you are a Christian and glad that there appears to be a Rapture of the Bride, remember there is major suffering and great "fear of what is to come" on Earth around the same time. Have empathy and love for the people of that time. Don't go praying that God brings that rapture forward, because you will be praying for the slaying of a fourth of the Earth's population by fighting, disease, famine, and wild beasts, great turmoil and pain for men, women, and children of all ages. Who would want to pray that forward?

Also, that section in Revelation 7:14 talks about the gathered coming *out* of the great tribulation, which could mean being actively removed *during* bad times, and not beforehand. Plenty of Christians have endured horrendous wars, famines, and diseases in the past—why would Christians of the future be a special case, avoid all trials and be removed in comfort?

Timeline Segment Summary: Time Block 3A

This is the revelation of Christ, when he returns to gather the Bride and take them back to his Father's house. The Bible repeatedly tells us *soon*, *quickly*, without warning so that we can understand that we are to be prepared. This is like waiting for the earthquake deemed The Big One in the West coast of Canada and the USA. We don't know when this mighty, life changing earthquake will happen, but we are supposed to prepare for it by tending to our supplies and have a plan in place. Yet few people actually do.

When is the mighty earthquake coming? Soon (geologically), quickly, and without warning.

When is the mighty Jesus coming? Soon (in historical terms), quickly, and without warning.

Once Jesus is revealed, it will be too late to do anything about his return. Just like trying to prepare for an earthquake when it is happening.

Here are the study passages to take a deeper look at Christ revealed:

* More Jewish Wedding analogies: John 3:27–29, Matthew 25:1–12
* The Sign of the Times: Joel 2:30–31, Luke 21:25–28, Revelation 6:12
* Jesus comes unexpectedly (be prepared): Matthew 24:36–44, Mark 13:32–37, Luke 17:26–30, Colossians 3:2–5, 1 Thessalonians 5:1–11, 1 Peter 1:13, Revelation 3:1–6
* Rapture: Revelation 7:9–17, Luke 17:31–36

Time Block 3A

- Mankind mourns over the Revealing of Christ: Isaiah 2:9–22, Revelation 6:13–17
- Satan ejected from Heaven to wreak havoc: Revelation 12:7–12
- Sealing of the 144 000 special Israelites before the destruction: Revelation 7:1–8, Zephaniah 3:13

Time Block 3B

Destruction of the Status Quo: Revelation 8, Revelation 12:7–12

The Time Block Overview													
The End Begins	Rise of the Modern World		Jesus Revealed [Day of the LORD]		The Three Terrors					Jesus Returns [Day of the LORD]		1 000-Year Reign		Judgment [Day of the LORD] and New Creation	
1	2		3		4					5		6		7	
A	A	B	A	B	A	B	C	D	E	A	B	A	B	A	B

Destruction of the Modern Way. (Performed Through Physical Means).

Whatever World-wide Cultures Exist—They End Here

There is no doubt in my mind that this Day of the Lord will wipe out whatever system, culture, and lifestyle we have in Modern Times. All destroyed by what can be called natural or man-made events.

At the signpost of the Black Sun/Red Moon, after the tribulations of Revelation 6:5–8, everything falls apart in a barrage of destructive fire, energy, and poison. There is an earthquake so great that "every island and mountain are moved from its place." The sky rolls apart by some great force. This must be an enormous event; the like of which humanity has never seen in person, but may well have occurred in the history of the world as a planet.

This is where the foundations of the upcoming evil kingdom are set down, growing from the desperate lives left behind; and yet this burst of destruction is not one of the three "Terrors" or "Woes" to follow. That illustrates how terrifying that which is about to happen in Time Blocks 4A–E must be.

It is not clear how long this destructive Time Block 3B lasts. A day? A week? No length of time is given, so it could even be a protracted period of years.

Yichud—or Period Alone

Certain Jewish communities identified as Ashkenazi have a ritual moment of quiet and seclusion in a special room for the Bride and Groom after the ceremony.[1] [2] This allows the Bride and Groom to have a moment's rest away from the excitement, and this seclusion was required to complete the wedding ceremony. This aligns nicely with the odd silence for half an hour in heaven after the 144 000 are sealed on Earth, and the multitude stand before Christ as his bride. Here Jesus (Lamb of God) completes the final breaking of all the seals on the scroll, which have caused all we have studied so far. See Revelation 8:1:

> When the Lamb broke the seventh seal on the scroll, there was silence throughout heaven for about half an hour. ^{NLT}

Note: other Jewish customs actually call Yichud a forbidden action between a man and an unmarried woman! So it does have more than one context. Keep that in mind.

The Wedding Feast parable also continues at this point, with the guests filling the banquet hall, waiting for the Bride and Groom to appear.

Revelation Continues with the Trumpets

After the seven seals culminate in the start of the tribulations, the Revealing of Christ, and the Rapture of the Bride, we have a particular event that

1. AICE, "*A Typical Ashkenazi Wedding Ceremony*"
2. Wikipedia, *Jewish Wedding*

happens repeatedly through Revelation: a Great Earthquake. This is a delineation between ends of events and the beginnings of worse.

After the particular earthquake of Revelation 8:5, we now come to seven Trumpets. Each one of these leads to a certain type of destruction, relentless in its nature. Here are the first four of Revelation 8:7–12:

> The first angel blew his trumpet, and hail and fire mixed with blood were thrown down on the earth. One-third of the earth was set on fire, one-third of the trees were burned, and all the green grass was burned.
>
> Then the second angel blew his trumpet, and a great mountain of fire was thrown into the sea. One-third of the water in the sea became blood, one-third of all things living in the sea died, and one-third of all the ships on the sea were destroyed.
>
> Then the third angel blew his trumpet, and a great star fell from the sky, burning like a torch. It fell on one-third of the rivers and on the springs of water. The name of the star was Bitterness. It made one-third of the water bitter, and many people died from drinking the bitter water.
>
> Then the fourth angel blew his trumpet, and one-third of the sun was struck, and one-third of the moon, and one-third of the stars, and they became dark. And one-third of the day was dark, and also one-third of the night. NLT

Revelation has been a classic fare for end-time studiers, fanatics, and conspiracy theorists with good reason: it describes events and creatures that are fantastical. We need to reflect on John's attempts to describe what he saw in his visions, many decades after Jesus's crucifixion. How would a man of that time (i.e., Roman Europe) describe a modern-day jet fighter or helicopter flying overhead? What noun would he use? Or how would he describe some of the advances in robotics?[3] Or a synchronized fleet of drones? How would he put into words *hypersonic missile, nuclear blast,* or *biological attack*? Or describe a large asteroid skimming the Earth's atmosphere?

People pooh-pooh John's vision, and I have even heard a Christian declare that John must have been on drugs. No, John was blessed with a vision from Lord Jesus himself. Jesus signs off the whole book with these spoken words of Revelation 22:16:

> "I, Jesus, have sent my angel to give you this message for the churches. I am both the source of David and the heir to his throne. I am the bright morning star." NLT

3. Boston Dynamics, *Introducing Handle*

As John was flooded with amazing images, he had few words to describe what he was seeing, so he did his best with the vocabulary and context he had available. As you read the next few paragraphs, I want you to know these are my own thoughts, for examples of how these trumpets could be played out in a natural disaster sense. This is not divine inspiration as far as I know.

For the first trumpet, the hail, fire, and blood raining down of the first destruction may refer to volcanic activity on a large scale. It also could be the result of a major impact with a celestial body, throwing burning rock into the sky, to rain back down as superheated beads. However the latter seems more like the second trumpet.

It takes only a small amount of imagination to replace the words "a great mountain thrown into the sea" due to the second trumpet with "asteroid"; and a star called bitterness (wormwood) that poisons a third of the fresh water to be also celestial. John saw the Wormwood star burn like a torch—surely in context with John's culture and history a torch would be more of a flaming, smoky burn, than a flash of a nuclear weapon?

The third of the stars, sun, and moon struck could mean a loss of light—but the Bible says it is "time based" more than "brightness based," with a third of the day missing, and likewise a third of the night (after all, how can the night be dark for a third, if it is already dark?). Does this mean eighteen hour days, rather than our current twenty-four hour days? My own thought on that (not Holy Spirit inspired) is an increased Earth rotation, possibly from the impacts of the mountain and wormwood!

The Second Angel of Revelation 14

As I mentioned before, the words of the three messengers that arrive in Revelation 14 can be pre-applied in part before that time.

With the trumpets and resultant horror wiping out everything we know, the second messenger's words (Revelation 14:8) can relate to the destruction of modern society. We talked of the typical prophecy of Babylon, which was a byword for a society or city seen to be completely against God's desires for us. This time it is the modern sick world of greed, poverty, lust, and slavery—not the ancient city already destroyed, nor the future seat of the world power that rises from the chaos.

Timeline Segment Summary—Time Block 3B

In the following study passages from the timeline, pay attention to the destruction of the modern world through physical and natural means, after Jesus goes back to his father's house with his bride. Most of this is in Revelation 8, but other prophets such as Isaiah and Zephaniah also describe typical prophecy that can relate to this period, as well as ancient history.

Even though the destruction is widespread and horrendous, all this is *before* the Terrors (or Woes) begin in force.

* The Jewish Wedding analogy continues: Matthew 22:10, Revelation 7:14—8:1

* Destruction of the Modern World begins: Isaiah 24:1-12, Isaiah 51:6, Zephaniah 1:1-13, Revelation 6:13-17, Revelation 8:5-12, Revelation 14:8

* Contrast the servants of God vs the rejecters of God: Isaiah 24:13-16, Isaiah 65:11-15, Proverbs 1:24-33

Time Block 4A

Terror One—The Destroyer's Locust Army: Revelation 9:1–11

The Time Block Overview						
The End Begins	Rise of the Modern World	Jesus Revealed [Day of the LORD]	The Three Terrors	Jesus Returns [Day of the LORD]	1 000-Year Reign	Judgment [Day of the LORD] and New Creation
1	2	3	4	5	6	7
A	A B	A B	A B C D E	A B	A B	A B

The First Terror: Strange Unearthly Attack.

The Start of the Terrors

In Revelation 8:13 we have a symbolic eagle warning the world of the terror that is about to engulf it. These three Terrors (or also translated as Woes) will continue until the Lord's return to Earth on the Day of the Lord in Time Block 5A as seen above.

With the start of Terror One, something much more sinister and personal replaces the proceeding natural world destruction of society in Time Block 3B. What comes next is distinctly supernatural and not explainable in normal terms.

The Destroyer (A.K.A. Abaddon)—Terror One

With world civilization now on fire, poisoned and destroyed by the events in Time Block 3B, the fifth Angel blows his commanding trumpet to introduce the Destroyer and his horrendous army.

This is one of those difficult to understand passages of Revelation, as the creatures described come from the smoke pouring from the abyss. The abyss itself is opened up by a star that falls from heaven to Earth; this star is given a pronoun "he" so this is an angel (or demon) given the authority to begin the terrors. The Destroyer is king over the other creatures within.

So who is The Destroyer?

Paul in 1 Corinthians 10:10 talks about those that the Destroyer killed in the past:

> We must not put Christ to the test, as some of them did and were destroyed by serpents, nor grumble, as some of them did and were destroyed by the Destroyer. ESV

This is also the Angel of Death in some Bible translations. Also, we have the destroyer mentioned in Exodus 12:23, in almost all English translations of the Bible. Again, the New Living Translation for instance declares the destroyer as God's death angel. Here is the English Standard Version translation:

> For the Lord will pass through to strike the Egyptians, and when he sees the blood on the lintel and on the two doorposts, the Lord will pass over the door and will not allow the destroyer to enter your houses to strike you. ESV

So in conclusion—The Destroyer is also translated as the Angel of Death and God's death angel.

If the previous Time Block 3B was nasty, this first Terror is appalling. With people reeling from the apparent natural or celestial disasters, plus the Wormwood incident, we now have attacks from creatures we can't fully understand as I write this, let alone what John could describe back in his day. Read Revelation 9:3-6.

The creatures appear like locusts, and their sole purpose seems to be to torment the entire remaining population of the Earth, with the exception of the 144 000 elect from before. Very oddly, there is no way to die from this torment no matter what you attempt, and there is a specific time allotted. Five months (150 days in Hebrew months).

Time Block 4A

John continues to describe what these locusts look like. I will leave it up to you to decide what you think they could be, but look at the way he describes them, using the knowledge of items he had the vocabulary for, in Roman occupied Judah (Revelation 9:7–11):

> The locusts looked like horses prepared for battle. They had what looked like gold crowns on their heads, and their faces looked like human faces. They had hair like women's hair and teeth like the teeth of a lion. They wore armor made of iron, and their wings roared like an army of chariots rushing into battle. They had tails that stung like scorpions, and for five months they had the power to torment people. Their king is the angel from the bottomless pit; his name in Hebrew is Abaddon, and in Greek, Apollyon—the Destroyer.[NLT]

With these creatures torturing mankind for five months, we come to the end of Terror One, and the beginning of Terror Two. What then, would be the mental state of anyone left from the destruction of the first trumpets, and the torture of the fifth? This is truly horrendous.

Timeline Segment Summary: Time Block 4A

See all we have studied for this supernatural attack in the following Bible passages:

* The Three Woes declared: Revelation 8:13
* The Abyss opened and Terror One released: Revelation 9:1–12, Isaiah 24:17,18
* The Destroyer King over the creatures from the Abyss: Job 28:22, Proverbs 16:4, Isaiah 54:16, Revelation 9:11

Time Block 4B

Terror Two—Gigantic Attack: Revelation 9:13-21, Revelation 13:1-4

The Time Block Overview														
The End Begins	Rise of the Modern World		Jesus Revealed [Day of the LORD]		The Three Terrors					Jesus Returns [Day of the LORD]		1 000-Year Reign		Judgment [Day of the LORD] and New Creation
1	2		3		4					5		6		7
A	A	B	A	B	A	B	C	D	E	A	B	A	B	A	B

The Second Terror: 200 Million Mounted Attackers.

The Second Terror Follows

The fantastical vision continues with four destroying angels turned loose with an army they may or may not command (this is not clear in some translations).[1] Revelation tells us that these four angels are currently bound at the great Euphrates River to be released to kill a third of mankind in Terror Two. This is accomplished through the "fire, smoke, and brimstone" plagues that come from the mouths of the "horses" the 200 million

---

1. Compare Revelation 9:16 in The New Living Translation, The Expanded Bible, The English Standard Version, King James Version and the New International Version to see how this is not too clear.

mounted troops ride. John likely related these creatures to a horse due to his vocabulary, but whatever they are, they resemble a horse figuratively (i.e., swift and powerful).

Whoever is left after the destruction wrought in Time Block 3B (after Jesus was revealed), remains alive in Time Block 4A (no death for five months) to face the 200 million mounted troops.

Who is the Unfortunate Remainder of Mankind?

Now would be a good time to put this into context. One of the difficult things about the end times, and specifically Revelation, is reconciling Jesus "The Lamb" with the same God who now allows such death and destruction. God loves us so much he was willing to sacrifice his own life, so we may join him at the Wedding, but now allows the 200 million troops to kill a third of mankind's remainder.

Jesus (God) *is* Love, but it is a fallacy to think he will tend, care, and protect you no matter what you do in his face; this is biblically inaccurate. Jesus warns us in the messages to the churches that there are expectations we have to *try* to meet. Anyone who has read the awful history of the Israelites' journey in the Old Testament will tell you that God is very patient, giving, and open to reconciliation, but there is a time for outright naughtiness to stop. When that happens, we get harsh lessons. God is patient, kind, and long-suffering for our benefit, but you just have to read the Bible to see (as with any parent) there is a line that we should not cross.

Jesus had, and has, immense patience with those who mocked, abused, rebuked, and continually conspired to kill him. But now, in the Terrors, Jesus has all dominion granted to him from the Father, and it is time for the final lesson.

What has happened recently in our history is the confusion between "the invite and free gift through unconditional love" with "I can spit in God's face and reject him, deny he even exists, and he'll still love me to the end." Yes, he *will* love you to the end, but he cannot stand un-holiness and will not let abject rejection to go unnoticed. This means God, in love, must be greatly saddened to have to stand back and allow a certain type of people get punished—punished because of how they totally reject him. God loves *us*, but not necessarily what we *do*.

Now, what of these poor people at the end, during the 200 million mounted army of death?

Quite possibly some wake up and declare they are in need of God's help, but look at Revelation 9:20–21:

> The rest of mankind, who were not killed by these plagues, did not repent of the works of their hands nor give up worshipping demons and idols of gold and silver and bronze and stone and wood, which cannot see or hear or walk nor did they repent of their murders or their sorceries or their sexual immorality or their thefts. ESV

Clearly the rest of mankind *did not* repent. No, they carried on without asking God for forgiveness, but digging in their heels and continuing what God declares not acceptable. Have a read and ponder this point—these people aren't worshipping demons and then crying out in honest sorrow to Jesus to help them reduce their devil worship. Nor are they being wholeheartedly sorry for their murders!

Are they fallen like I am? Yes.

Are they trying not to be? No.

Does God love them as much as he does me? *Yes, unconditionally!*

Will he accept this behavior? No, never! For he is holy.

I hope this helps you understand how a God that loves us unconditionally is also the Holiest of Holies and cannot allow outright, deliberate, passionate unholy behavior to be separated from the words *try not to*. He loves us, but there are consequences for what we do, otherwise, how can we ever learn?

Fear of the Lord is the beginning of Wisdom—the Bible says that in Psalm 111:10. Fear does not mean shrinking fright from a possible psychotic attack; fear means reverence and respect for a God so mighty and holy he cannot *stand* unholy, so please remember that. This is why he sent his one and only son: to wipe everyone's un-holiness away, the instant he died on the cross in place of us. If you understand the depth of that action (for he initiated that sacrifice for us, not the other way around), you should be humbled.

Read Psalm 25. God will be your friend, but you have a place with respect to authority, and so does he. Here is Verse 3:

> Indeed, none who wait for you shall be put to shame; they shall be ashamed who are wantonly treacherous. ESV

He is the authority above all, the creator not the created. Respect that, revere who God is, and he'll be your friend and tutor. That is too much to ask of some people, who would stiffen their neck and say, "if he wants to be *my* friend, he should sort *my* life out/give *me* a million dollars/end world suffering/help *me* get what I want" and so on.

In conclusion, these last peoples of the world who face such repeated devastation are wild, uncontrolled, murderous, violent, lusty, demonic worshippers. If they asked Jesus for forgiveness with a contrite heart, and admitted he is Lord, what would Jesus do?

Forgive them, of course!

But they don't. Could it be that they have already pledged allegiance with the other side? Satan's world and Satan's ways? And wholeheartedly rejected God?

The Beginnings of the Fourth Kingdom

From the death and destruction wrought from Terror 1 and Terror 2, and the sort of people we see in Revelation 9:20-21 left behind, a new power emerges—violent and strong. Daniel 7:23 and Revelation 13:1-4 mention this. Here is Daniel:

> Then he said to me, "This fourth beast is the fourth world power that will rule the earth. It will be different from all the others. It will devour the whole world, trampling and crushing everything in its path." NLT

And Revelation 13:1-2:

> Then I saw a beast rising up out of the sea. It had seven heads and ten horns, with ten crowns on its horns. And written on each head were names that blasphemed God. This beast looked like a leopard, but it had the feet of a bear and the mouth of a lion! And the dragon gave the beast his own power and throne and great authority. NLT

Note that Satan gives this kingdom its power, throne, and authority. This tells us what that kingdom is going to be like: deluding, violent, self-serving, and do anything you want to without caring. You may think this sounds great as there is no finger wagging God to teach, rebuke and guide you away from wanton self-absorbed enjoyment and desires, but Satan does not relinquish authority to humanity. It isn't free anarchy and no more government controlled societies. A different authority will force and delude humanity do what Satan wants it to do: worship Satan as a god, and not the true God. See Revelation 13:4:

> They worshipped the dragon for giving the beast such power, and they also worshipped the beast. "Who is as great as the beast?" they exclaimed. "Who is able to fight against him?" NLT

Ten kings will run this new kingdom from the chaos. Just how long these kings take to grab power and subdue the world's leftover population is not too clear, but by Time Block 4C it will be in full effect.

A new Babylon type city is also linked to this crushing kingdom, and Satan's kingdom carries (supports) this city until such times as it is no longer needed. We will look at this later in the book.

Timeline Segment Summary: Time Block 4B

See the verses that follow, for a more in-depth look at the segment of the timeline that deals with the Second Terror's beginning.

- 200 million troops kill a third of the remainder: Revelation 9:13–19
- The Rise of the fourth and final world power: Daniel 7:7 & 23–25, Revelation 13:1–4
- A new city emerges (as a foundation for the Beast Kingdom): Revelation 9:20–21

Interlude—A Brief Explanation of The Beasts

The Angel of Death, Beast from the Sea, Beast from the Earth, Abomination of Desolation

It wouldn't be an End Times Study without the usual delve into the Beast, Final Kingdoms, Antichrists, and so on. So, for the purposes of clarifying what wisdom the Holy Spirit granted me, here is a brief look of the major bad guys to help you in the following Time Blocks.

The Angel of The Pit (Abyss) "Abaddon" or Angel of Death

This is Abaddon (The Destroyer), whom we have already met as he is king over the locust army. Whether he is king of the four destroying angels is not revealed. Remember he is also God's Angel of Death and has been around throughout history, see page 60.

Beast from the Sea: Revelation 13:1–3

Some confusion exists with this beast: is the Beast from the sea a King or a Kingdom? Daniel 7:3, along with Daniel 7:7, Daniel 7:23 and Revelation 13:1–3, says the fourth beast is one of four that rise from the stirred-up sea—but in context are *kingdoms*. However, in Daniel 7:17 the Bible states these kingdoms arise from the Earth.

To help clarify, here is what happens: firstly, a Beast Kingdom rises from the sea (and chaos of the Terrors) and then a specific King rises to take control of it, as described in Daniel 7:24 and Revelation 17:11–13 (see later in this section).

So, in conclusion the Beast of Revelation 13:1–3 *is both* a kingdom system, as well as a particular person. Both inseparable as one evil entity.

Have a read of Daniel 2:31–45 to see the complete description of the four kingdoms, given as a dream to King Nebuchadnezzar and interpreted by Daniel through God's wisdom. Here are verses 40 – 42:

> Following that kingdom, there will be a fourth one, as strong as iron. That kingdom will smash and crush all previous empires, just as iron smashes and crushes everything it strikes. The feet and toes you saw were a combination of iron and baked clay, showing that this kingdom will be divided. Like iron mixed with clay, it will have some of the strength of iron. But while some parts of it will be as strong as iron, other parts will be as weak as clay. NLT

Also, in Daniel 9:26 second sentence, there is a mention that the "people of the prince who is to come" are the ones who destroyed the city and sanctuary, which almost certainly relates to the destruction of Jerusalem in AD 70 at the hands of the Roman Empire. However, in typical prophecy manner it also links to the type of the last great kingdom that will rule the Earth at the end, i.e., like a Roman Empire—swift, crushing, brutal.

Satan (the Dragon) gives authority and power to the Beast Kingdom and Beast King. Indeed, John tells us that people worship Satan due to Satan giving his power to the Beast Kingdom. They also worship the Beast Kingdom as they say, "who can fight against it"? Once again, the analogies to the Roman Empire, and even the Nazi conquests of the early part of the Second World War, are very apparent.

Now, about that Beast King, also known as the "Little Horn" and "Man of Lawlessness."

Daniel in Daniel 7:8 and Daniel 7:20, as well as John in Revelation 13:3–6, tells us a distinct mouthpiece figurehead forms part of the Beast Kingdom. Here is verse 5 of the Revelation 13 passage:

> And the beast was given a mouth uttering haughty and blasphemous words, and it was allowed to exercise authority for forty-two months. ESV

This is also described symbolically in Revelation 12:15 as a flood of water from the Dragon's mouth.

Revelation 17:9–13 describes this head of the kingdom quite mystically. Here an angel tells John that the seven heads are the seven hills the Great Prostitute (new Babylon) sits on, but also the seven heads are seven

Interlude—A Brief Explanation of The Beasts

kings. And here's where you'll need to pray for discernment, as the angel says:

> This calls for a mind with wisdom: the seven heads are seven mountains on which the woman is seated; they are also seven kings, five of whom have fallen, one is, the other has not yet come, and when he does come he must remain only a little while. As for the beast that was and is not, it is an eighth but it belongs to the seven, and it goes to destruction. And the ten horns that you saw are ten kings who have not yet received royal power, but they are to receive authority as kings for one hour, together with the beast. These are of one mind, and they hand over their power and authority to the beast. ^{ESV}

Here is what I understand, after reading a whole collection of Bible passages about this beast and the Beast Kingdom, in reverse order (as it is easier to understand from that direction):

At the end, ten *new* kings do the bidding of the Beast Kingdom, and these are the ten horns of Revelation 17:12. These ten kings are voluntarily subject to the authority of the Beast King, who was the eighth of a succession to take power, such that the ten new kings rule under the direction of the Head.

If we go back one step from this final structure of the Kingdom, dictated by one head with ten powers, there is a set of kings that comes before the Eighth different king. It seems there were supposed to be ten of these original kings, but when the Eighth appears that all changes. These successive kings are associated with the early Beast Kingdom and seem to be the foundation, which would suggest a succession of kings rising during Terror Two. This succession of kings are the seven heads. Clear so far?

Five of these successive heads fall. One, in context with the time the angel is discussing, is alive and active. This is number six in succession. One more (number seven) is to follow but won't be around for long before the Beast king turns up. The other three that were supposed to be rulers never happen because of what the Little Horn does in Daniel 7:8 and here in Daniel 7:20:

> I also asked about the ten horns on the fourth beast's head and the little horn that came up afterward and destroyed three of the other horns. This horn had seemed greater than the others, and it had human eyes and a mouth that was boasting arrogantly. ^{NLT}

So, those "five were, one is and one to come" are the seven heads of Revelation 13:1.

> Then I saw a beast rising up out of the sea. It had seven heads and ten horns, with ten crowns on its horns. And written on each head were names that blasphemed God. ^{NLT}

I hope you are understanding this so far, for next we have the more mysterious message from Revelation 17:8: there is the eighth king that is one of the seven but *"was, and is not, and is about to rise from the bottomless pit and go to destruction."* This sounds bizarre. How can there be seven heads, and then an eighth head that is not part of the Beast Kingdom of Revelation 13:1?

Consider this: Daniel 7:24 says he will be different to the other ten kings and will subdue three of the first kings. If you read Daniel 7:7–8 there were ten horns, but another arises and tears out three of the original horns to make room for it. So, we are back to seven plus the odd eighth little horn.

Revelation 13:3 states that one of the *heads* has a mortal wound, but is healed. Revelation 17:8 clarifies the beast was dead, but is alive, and reappears.

Therefore, one of five successive kings that have fallen (died), turns up again, *resurrected and powered by Satan*. This re-animated demonic king then subdues three original kings and takes full control of the kingdom. He then has a new set of kings installed (ten of them), and these willingly do his bidding. This suggests a dictator with ten heads of either states, jurisdictions, or regions, but no real power of their own.

The angel of Revelation reminds us that this final state of affairs is not for long though, hence the angel stating an hour. A short period, not a literal hour as we will see later.

For those that want to study this confusing Beast of Revelation 13:1–10 and decide for themselves how it all fits together—here are all the passages I read and studied:

* Daniel 7:7–8, 11, Daniel 7:20–25, Daniel 12:11
* Second Thessalonians 2:1–12
* Revelation 13:1–10, Revelation 14:9–11, Revelation 15:2, Revelation 16:1–16, Revelation 17, Revelation 20:10

Interlude—A Brief Explanation of The Beasts

The Beast from the Earth: Revelation 13:11-14

Now we (hopefully) understand the first beast as being a blend of kingdom and special re-animated king; who then is the second beast from the Earth in Revelation 13:11?

This beast is the Antichrist or False Prophet.

This person exercises all the authority of the Beast King, and he can do remarkable things powered by Satan: miracles and fire from Heaven according to John in Revelation 13:12; and he forces *everyone* to worship the Beast (King).

This False Prophet deceives all the people that belong to this world. That means, everyone who rejects God, for you are either of God or of the World. Then, he orders people to make the Abomination of Desolation statue of the Beast King (the one with the mortal wound that healed—the Little Horn).

What happens next is no longer far-fetched in our current modern times, based on the remarkable strides in Artificial Intelligence and robotics: The False Prophet then gives "breath" to this statue so that it can fulfill its terrible purpose, as it seems to come alive.

The Abomination of Desolation: Matthew 24:15

Jesus points us to Daniel when he is telling his disciples about the end times. Jesus's words are in Matthew 24:15, and Daniel 12:11 is where you will find what Jesus was talking about. This Abomination of Desolation actually has a historical place too—as a Greek persecutor of the Jewish race called Antiochus IV Epiphanes. He desecrated the Temple of God with a statue of Zeus, and this sort of desecration seems to be a pattern.[1]

As mentioned before, the False Prophet orders people into making an image (idol) of the Beast Kingdom's final figurehead, which is the "head with the fatal wound that lived." However, this idol then becomes the Abomination of Desolation when it is animated and placed in the Temple of Jerusalem as a way to desecrate God's holy space and people.

So for us, the Abomination of Desolation is the animated statue of the Beast, telling everyone what to do and forcing them to have that infamous mark: the name of the Beast King, or the number of its name—666 (or 616 depending on other manuscripts); this being the number of a man. I'm

---

1. Wikipedia, *Abomination of Desolation*

not going into who the man is, or whether 666 is the actual mark. What is important is that the animated Beast-King-figurehead-image is the thing that forces people to have the mark and worship the image of the Beast, or be slain.

Note: the word *beast* is used so much it can be confusing to know which "beast" the statue forces people to worship: the Antichrist or the Beast King? According to 2 Thessalonians 2:3–10, and Revelation 13:14–15 it is the Man of Lawlessness, the beast that was "wounded by the sword yet lived." So, this is the Beast King.

This action of placing the Abomination of Desolation in the temple, and the enforced worship of the first Beast and his image as a god is the beginning of the end for Satan's empire, as God begins the countdown to when he comes back and shows the world who *actually* is in charge.

For reference, I believe one of the temple desecrations of the past fulfilled the following passages and so does not apply to our journey into the End Times:

* Daniel 9:24–27
* Daniel 11:29–45

The Dragon: Revelation 12:3

In Revelation 12:3 we see a great red dragon having seven heads and ten horns. This is Satan, in *symbolic* form. How do I know? Because the Bible tells us in Revelation 12:9.

Note: Satan is described in a couple of places as a dragon, and is not the scarlet *beast* described in Revelation 17:3. Instead, think of the *type* of Beast Kingdom described in Revelation 17:3 as being of the type "Satanic."

The description in Revelation 12:3 has led to imagery that Satan is a red demonic looking fellow. However, in the classic address to Satan in the Bible (Ezekiel 28:11–19), which begins as funeral song to the King of Tyre, Satan is described as "a model of perfection, full of wisdom and exquisite in beauty."

If the world believes he is an ugly, terrible looking, red dragon, this is just the sort of deception that he uses to his advantage. People will likely believe a bright shiny glorious being is good, whereas an ugly leathery thing is bad. Just remember, Revelation 12 is very symbolic, not literal.

Interlude—A Brief Explanation of The Beasts

Satan is a beautiful (but not *lovely*) guardian cherub that the Holy Spirit warns us to respect, not mock. Don't worship, don't agree with, don't listen to Satan, but do respect him for the mighty guardian cherubim he is. The Bible describes him as a roaring lion, looking to devour us. The *only* defense we have against him is God residing in us, who guards us as our and Satan's King. Without Jesus and the Holy Spirit sent by the Father in us, we are on our own against a mighty guardian cherub and personally, as a rather cowardly fellow, I have no desire for that. Respect the dangerous creature, and don't be foolish.

Interestingly, if God is our only defense, this also shows Satan's power is not the opposite of God's; The Father, Jesus and the Holy Spirit have absolutely no trouble controlling and rebuking him. Therefore—if you welcome Jesus into your heart, you too can rebuke Satan. Jude tells us how in Jude 8 – 9; "the Lord rebuke you!" with respect at the sort of being Satan is. Do not mock, thinking you are more powerful. Even Michael the Archangel used those words according to Jude, and I know you are nowhere near as powerful as an Archangel. "The Lord rebuke you." That's it. Nothing more is needed.

The Beast we studied before cannot be Satan, even though both are symbolically described as having Seven Heads, Diadems and Ten Horns (read Revelation 12:3 and Revelation 13:1). So then, why can they not be the same?

The answer lies later on, during a big battle; here the Beast is destroyed and Satan captured simultaneously, chained for a thousand years. There is a lot of blurring between the two, as Satan powers the Beast Kingdom and the final King. In a way, it is like they are overlaid on top of each other so they are inseparable, and yet distinct, maybe even like putting two circles on top of each other on one page?

To assist in seeing this overlay between Satan and the Beast King, we should take a brief backwards look using Revelation 17:8, where an angel discusses the beast:

> The beast that you saw was, and is not, and is about to rise from the bottomless pit and go to destruction. And the dwellers on earth whose names have not been written in the book of life from the foundation of the world will marvel to see the beast, because it was and is not and is to come." ESV

The Dragon is the source of both the final kingdom and the resurrected Beast King. We can see a parallel between what happened to the Beast

King (died with a mortal wound, yet rose again as healed to become the Man of Lawlessness, and ends up going to destruction when Jesus returns) with what is also going to happen to Satan. He also once was (Revelation 12:3, 9), is no longer (Revelation 12:10–12) and will rise from the bottomless pit (goes into the pit in Revelation 20:1–3, and comes out in Revelation 20:7) and go to his destruction (Revelation 20:10).

In conclusion, the Bible uses very similar symbolic ways to describe the first Beast and Satan, which can lead to confusion. Just imagine them overlaid and transparent, so each show through the other, and that will probably help.

Time Block 4C–4E

Terror Two and Three—The Beast Kingdom and Its Ruler: A Complete Overview

The Time Block Overview												
The End Begins	Rise of the Modern World	Jesus Revealed [Day of the LORD]	The Three Terrors				Jesus Returns [Day of the LORD]		1 000-Year Reign		Judgment [Day of the LORD] and New Creation	
1	2	3	4				5		6		7	
A	A	B	A	B	A	B	C	D	E	A	B	A	B	A	B

The Second and Third Terrors: The Fourth World Kingdom and the Mouthpiece King.

The Signs and Times of the Final World Order

From the overview above, you can see that the Beast Forth World Kingdom spans the second and third Terrors and is sandwiched between two Day of the Lords of Jesus.

If you look at the persecution driven by misguided individuals today, you might wonder if we are not already in the final world order; but the Beast Kingdom controls the *whole* world, and at the time of writing most of the Western world has more comfort and first world issues than there is outright brutal persecution. Persecution does exist, yes, but nowhere near the scale of this final kingdom on Earth. That should worry you, and yet comfort you, knowing you still have time left to avoid that final state of evil authority.

Take note of what Paul says in 2 Thessalonians 2:1–12; if you didn't study it previously (page 72) here is the salient point in verses 1–3:

> Now, dear brothers and sisters, let us clarify some things about the coming of our Lord Jesus Christ and how we will be gathered to meet him. Don't be so easily shaken or alarmed by those who say that the Day of the Lord has already begun. Don't believe them, even if they claim to have had a spiritual vision, a revelation, or a letter supposedly from us. Don't be fooled by what they say. For that day will not come until there is a great rebellion against God and the man of lawlessness is revealed—the one who brings destruction. NLT

Here he is calming people and telling them that there is a certain distinct order of things; and the lawless one has to be revealed and do his works first, before the Day of the Lord in Time Block 5A.

Clearly the technology exists to produce a mark of the beast that you can use to buy food and goods. Simply implant an RFI tag into your hand, then use a reader to check if you can buy food, and there you go, purchase made. However, just because we have many technological methods to copy the Beast's world order, there are distinct reasons why we are not there yet. In a summary:

1. Jesus will be revealed to the whole world beforehand, and no one is going to miss that event.
2. There is a massive undeniable destruction of the whole world after Jesus's revelation.
3. Two hundred million mounted troops of unearthly origin then go through the world killing a third of mankind.
4. There needs to be a third temple in Jerusalem (see Revelation 11:1–2), so that the Abomination of Desolation has a place to be set up. At the time of writing there has only been two temples.

There is no evidence to say that we are currently in the Beast World Kingdom. Things around us may imitate it closely, especially as human nature repeats itself throughout history, but look at what should have all happened first and then take an educated guess at where you think we are.

Time Block 4C–4E

Daniel, Revelation, and the Time Periods

For this Beast Kingdom, there are studied verses from Daniel and Revelation, and we should see a distinct correlation between the two. They are both talking about the same thing, especially the rise and fall of the Beast Kingdom, so there should be *no disagreements* between Daniel and Revelation.

The most difficult part of this turned out to be the periods of 1 260 days and 1 290 days mentioned by Daniel and Revelation. You will find the 1 260 day period called 42 months, Time, Times, and Half a Time, and 1 260 days. Here is a quick summary of each period, before we look at each in detail in the coming Time Blocks:

The first 1 260 days – Time Block 4C: this is the protection of the remnant of Israel from the mouthpiece of the Beast Kingdom as he subdues three Horn powers and takes command of everything. It is during this period that Revelation 11:1–14 occurs. Also Revelation 12:6 and 14 describe this, both shown below:

> ... and the woman fled into the wilderness, where she has a place prepared by God, in which she is to be nourished for 1,260 days.
>
> ... But the woman was given the two wings of the great eagle so that she might fly from the serpent into the wilderness, to the place where she is to be nourished for a time, and times, and half a time. ᴱˢⱽ

The Second 1 260 days – Time Block 4D: At this time the Antichrist (False Prophet) sets up the statue Abomination of Desolation in the Third Temple (see Revelation 13:14–15) triggering the final count down.

The Beast Kingdom then goes to war against God's true followers, overcoming them as per Daniel 7:21:

> As I looked, this horn made war with the saints and prevailed over them. ᴱˢⱽ

As well as Daniel 12:7:

> And I heard the man clothed in linen, who was above the waters of the stream; he raised his right hand and his left hand toward heaven and swore by him who lives forever that it would be for a time, times, and half a time, and that when the shattering of the power of the holy people comes to an end all these things would be finished. ᴱˢⱽ

And Revelation 13:7

> Also it was allowed to make war on the saints and to conquer them. And authority was given it over every tribe and people and language and nation... ᴱˢⱽ

The Final 30 Days – Time Block 4E: from Daniel 9:27 and Daniel 12:7, we know that the time of the final Beast Kingdom is split equally into two halves. One-half of a week of seven Hebrew years equates to 1 260 days, as does a "time, times and half a time". Here is Daniel 9:27:

> And he shall make a strong covenant with many for one week, and for half of the week he shall put an end to sacrifice and offering. And on the wing of abominations shall come one who makes desolate, until the decreed end is poured out on the desolator. ᴱˢⱽ

However, an angel also tells Daniel the time of the Abomination of Desolation lasts for 1 290 days in Daniel 12:11.

This would mean that there is one Hebrew month between the end of the final 1 260 days of the Beast Kingdom, and the return of Christ as the victor in Time Block 5A.

This thirty day span is the duration of the seven bowls of God's wrath of Time Block 4E. I will cover this in more detail as we dive into the three distinct Time Blocks of the Beast World Kingdom.

First up is the Beast Kingdom leader taking full control.

Time Block 4C

Terror Two Continues—A New King Rules: Revelation 11:1–14, Revelation 12:6, Revelation 12:13–16, Revelation 13:5–6, Revelation 17:1–10, 18

The Time Block Overview							
The End Begins	Rise of the Modern World	Jesus Revealed [Day of the LORD]	The Three Terrors			Jesus Returns [Day of the LORD]	1 000-Year Reign	Judgment [Day of the LORD] and New Creation
1	2	3	4			5	6	7
A	A | B	A | B	A | B | C | D | E			A | B	A | B	A | B

The Second Terror—Beast Kingdom (under 4: A \| B)

The New World Kingdom and a New Babylon

From the total societal collapse in Terror One and the beginning of Terror Two, coupled with the understanding of what the people on Earth look like in terms of civilisation (see Revelation 9:20–21), we now see the formation of a new world order. This is the start of Daniel's Fourth World Kingdom seen in Daniel 7:23.

A new Babylon city rises on the back of this kingdom, as described in Revelation 17. Here is verse 3:

> And he carried me away in the Spirit into a wilderness, and I saw a woman sitting on a scarlet beast that was full of blasphemous names, and it had seven heads and ten horns. ᴱˢⱽ

The woman is the new city (this will be shown later); and what of the beast that the city sits on? As we saw on pages 69 and 70, the Beast Kingdom's symbolic form has seven heads and ten horns.

The descriptions of what this city will be like continue in Revelation 17:4–6:

> The woman was arrayed in purple and scarlet, and adorned with gold and jewels and pearls, holding in her hand a golden cup full of abominations and the impurities of her sexual immorality. And on her forehead was written a name of mystery: "Babylon the great, mother of prostitutes and of earth's abominations." And I saw the woman, drunk with the blood of the saints, the blood of the martyrs of Jesus. ᴱˢⱽ

This tells us it will be full of luxuries and wealth, but also darkly evil and sexually promiscuous (like the Roman Empire). Interestingly, our present-day Western media and stories tend to contain sexual promiscuity and violence, because it sells very well. With the new Babylon city, Satan plays humanity's basic traits like a well-tuned instrument in his hands.

There is a common theory this prostitute described is actually a new world religion based heavily on Roman Catholicism. Admittedly, there is a lot of symbolism that may suggest this (colors, wealth), but at the end of passage, in Revelation 17:18, this notion is nullified by the Angel saying clearly, "The Woman you saw (prostitute) in your vision represents the great city." Not a religion, but a city. Could be a city-state? Perhaps there is a new religion associated strongly with this city?

Now here is some human wisdom that I can't escape from and is widely known today: the Angel tells us that this city sits on seven mountains, or hills according to some translations. So, this points strongly to old Rome, due to the Seven Hills of Rome. Coupled with this is the contextual description that fits within the period of John, writing what he saw in his vision. At that time, Rome was the center of a crushing empire and anyone reading John's writings would understand this context of a great city riding on the back of a violent empire.

Why Babylon? Recall that throughout the Bible the name Babylon is used for any society or city that is really bad, cruel, and displeasing to God—no doubt based on what Babylon of old was like as a city, and as a society. So, we have a doubly bad connection here: Old Rome and Old Babylon combined as a type of city and society we can expect the Beast Kingdom to generate.

Interestingly, the infamous Beast Kingdom carries this city to allow it to grow, get rich, powerful, and very corrupt by the kings that run the kingdom. However, waiting in the wings is another King. Satan will be behind this particular king to fulfill Satan's ultimate goal, which does not end well for this city, nor anyone on the Earth (including the 144 000).

The Third Temple Must Exist

After the Romans destroyed the Temple in AD 70, there has not been a successful rebuild to the present day (as I write this).

As mentioned before on page 76—the existence of this Third Temple is important as we carry on through the Time Blocks, as the Book of Revelation mentions the interaction between the Beast, the Antichrist, and the temple, as well as Jesus coming to reign on Earth, residing in a temple in Time Block 5A and 5B. Therefore, if there is no third temple, then none of this can come to pass. It is that simple.

The Two Witnesses and the Little Horn

Another major event in the continuation of Terror Two, after the 200 million troops kill a third of mankind, is a remarkable verbal battle between two mysterious witnesses of the Lord and the mouthpiece of the Beast Kingdom.

During this time, the Gentiles (that's anyone not an Israelite) trample Jerusalem as the Little Horn does a mass spewing of propaganda against God and anyone in heaven. However, at the same time two witnesses stand and prophesy to the world, sending fire "flashing from their mouths" against any peoples or person who would try and harm them. They can also bring plagues and droughts to the earth as often as they wish.

This flashing fire is probably symbolic of the power of their words (from their mouths). For example, elsewhere you will read about Jesus having a sword coming from his mouth—the two-edged sword of the Word of

God. So, not a literal sword, but instead the effects and power are described. Same for the two witnesses.

I would have to guess at what the two witnesses are saying, but I suspect it is the complete opposite of what the Little Horn Beast King is saying.

Who are these two witnesses? In ancient history, God took Elijah and Enoch from the Earth without them dying, which could be a clue. However, Moses could also be a contender for being one of the witnesses, as he and Elijah appear with Jesus in front of Peter, James, and John in Luke 9:30–31:

> Suddenly, two men, Moses and Elijah, appeared and began talking with Jesus. They were glorious to see. And they were speaking about his exodus from this world, which was about to be fulfilled in Jerusalem. NLT

Who the two witnesses are in Revelation 11 is not important. After all, John was there on the mountain in the passage above and described a definite Moses and Elijah; and yet when he describes the two witnesses in Revelation 11, he does not reveal their identity.

What is important is that the Little Horn King kills them after they have finished their message. Only to find, three and a half days later, they ascend like Jesus at the command of a loud voice from Heaven and go up in a cloud!

As mentioned on page 77, the 144 000 Israelites are protected during this time in a place in the wilderness as described by Revelation 12:6 and Revelation 12:13–14. Therefore, the Two Witnesses occur during the first forty-two Hebrew months (or 1 260 days) of Daniels week of years.

After the ascension of the two witnesses, a great earthquake occurs and a terrified population of the city of Jerusalem give glory to God. Interestingly, the terrified population admit God did it, admit there *is* God, even give him glory for it—but still don't seem to repent. What sort of people are these? Perhaps the ones that are fully deluded that Satan is their only savior and true power.

Note: the Bible declares that after the witnesses and earthquake, Terror Two has passed, but the third Terror is soon to come. This means the transition between Terror Two and Terror Three is right in the middle of the two 1 260 day periods of Time Block 4C and 4D.

Time Block 4C

Timeline Segment Summary: Time Block 4C

Scripture documents this Time Block well, with Daniel and Revelation intertwined in the events. Here are the more in-depth scriptures to look at.

- A different king arises: Daniel 7:8, Daniel 7:24, 2 Thessalonians 2:3–4 & 9–12, Revelation 13:11–13, Revelation 17:10–13
- A new greed and lust-based Rome/Babylon, powered by Satan: Revelation 17:1–9 & 15
- Two witnesses in a verbal battle with the Little Horn (Eighth king): Zechariah 4:11–14, Malachi 4:5, Revelation 11:1–4, Revelation 12:15–16, Revelation 13:5–6
- The 144 000 are nourished and protected during this time: Revelation 12:6, Revelation 12:13–14

Time Block 4D

Terror 3—Mark of the Beast and Abomination of Desolation: Revelation 13:7–10, Revelation 13:11–18, Revelation 17:12–18, Revelation 18

The Time Block Overview							
The End Begins	Rise of the Modern World	Jesus Revealed [Day of the LORD]	The Three Terrors			Jesus Returns [Day of the LORD]	1 000-Year Reign	Judgment [Day of the LORD] and New Creation
1	2	3	4			5	6	7
A	A | B	A | B	A | B | C | D | E			A | B	A | B	A | B

The Third Terror—Beast Kingdom: Abomination of Desolation.

A Time Given By Jesus (Spoken by Daniel)

Start the clock! Here is an actual timestamp from God himself. Read what he says in Matthew 24:15–18 and 22:

> "So when you see the abomination of desolation spoken of by the prophet Daniel, standing in the holy place (let the reader understand), then let those who are in Judea flee to the mountains. Let the one who is on the housetop not go down to take what is in his house, and let the one who is in the field not turn back to take his cloak.

Time Block 4D

> ... And if those days had not been cut short, no human being would be saved. But for the sake of the elect those days will be cut short." ᴱˢⱽ

The "let the reader understand" is possibly the only place where God breaks the fourth wall for us in the Bible. It stands out to me in this passage. It is a personal message to us, reading his word thousands of years after he spoke them and inspired the writer to add those parentheses. Here Jesus gives a royal seal on Daniel's prophecy in Daniel 12:11:

> "From the time the daily sacrifice is stopped and the sacrilegious object that causes desecration is set up to be worshipped, there will be 1,290 days." ᴺᴸᵀ

When the False Prophet beast sets up the Abomination of Desolation (living statue), this is the start of Terror Three. A truly horrendous time. Anyone left reading the Bible will know they only have to survive another 1 290 days before Jesus returns on the Great and Terrible Day of The Lord; and then, interestingly, make it to 1 335 days to get a great blessing.

A Terrible Time for All Who Follow God, and For All That Don't

After the 1 260 days of protection given to the 144 000 Israelites and any new followers of Jesus, (previously in Time Block 4C), we now come to a violent time of utter persecution for these souls. They are broken, as described in Revelation 13:7–10 and cannot fight back. Here are verses 7 (in part) and 8–10:

> And the beast was allowed to wage war against God's holy people and to conquer them ...
> ... Anyone with ears to hear should listen and understand.
> Anyone who is destined for prison will be taken to prison.
> Anyone destined to die by the sword will die by the sword.
> This means that God's holy people must endure persecution patiently and remain faithful. ᴺᴸᵀ

There is *no other option* but to die by the sword or end up in prison. Remember this persecution lasts for three and a half years. As the Bible says: It calls for perseverance and faith of the saints.

This is the moment in history where the short-lived Beast Kingdom of the Little Horn, ten kings and the Antichrist takes control of everything; with every nation, tribe, tongue and people given over to it. As Satan powers this kingdom of the World, one could say this is the culmination of all his efforts. This is the climax of his plans he had for us, which speaks volumes about who Satan is.

It is also the point in time where the Beast Kingdom snarls up at the Prostitute city that believes it has control and power. Not anymore. The city is destroyed as described in Revelation 18.

The Beast Kingdom, with its figurehead Beast King, Antichrist and animated Abomination of Desolation statue, now have world domination with no one in the way—except God.

The Number of the Beast: 666

Hands up anyone in the Western world that has *not* heard of that number? Some manuscripts have it as 616.

With the Beast King in total control, the Antichrist rises and speaks with mightiness, causes all to worship the Beast and set up a statue and make it speak! After this, with Jesus's clock now ticking down the 1 290 days, the *statue* forces everyone to receive a mark on their right hand or forehead, without which you will starve and be destitute.

It is interesting how the dead statue does this, and not the Beast King or Antichrist. The mark forced upon people is one of two things:

1. The name of the Beast—which is the Man of Lawlessness or Little Horn.
2. The number of the Beast that represents his name. This is the "666" (or maybe "616").

What does 666 mean? People have said many, many things (just search on the internet, you won't be short of answers); but again, I plead with you—it doesn't matter who or what 666 comes up with as a name—what is important is that you know who your savior is, and what he did for you.

If you are currently in a world solely controlled by a violent dictator and other puppet kings/powers, with a talking idol giving commands, don't accept *any* mark! Those people who accept the mark truly have no hope, as they have instantly damned themselves to the same fate as Death, The Grave, and Satan.

This leads to a gray area; if you unwillingly have that mark forced upon you, have you *accepted* it? You'll know in your heart, and so will God of course. See what the third angel of Revelation 14:9–11 has to say, and

Time Block 4D

ask for your own Holy Spirit wisdom about what constitutes accepting the mark:

> Then a third angel followed them, shouting, "Anyone who worships the beast and his statue or who accepts his mark on the forehead or on the hand must drink the wine of God's anger. It has been poured full strength into God's cup of wrath. And they will be tormented with fire and burning sulfur in the presence of the holy angels and the Lamb. The smoke of their torment will rise forever and ever, and they will have no relief day or night, for they have worshipped the beast and his statue and have accepted the mark of his name." NLT

If there is any doubt at all in your mind about what constitutes acceptance, it is truly better to die once at the hands of the Beast Kingdom and followers and live eternally, than to die once and then die twice eternally.

Once again, I want to remind you that modern technology and endless conspiracy theories do not mean we are in the Beast Kingdom part of the End Times. Yes, right now humanity could generate a mark on you that is readable. However, look around and see the truth in the scripture. In 2022, we were not there. Are you? In whatever year you are reading this in? Is there a talking statue controlling the world? From a Third Temple in Jerusalem? Do you remember the 200 million mounted troops? Not to mention those five months of no death but pain through demonic locust attack?

Also—has it been *more than* 1 260 + 1 290 days since whomever the conspiracy theorists declare the antichrist is has appeared? If so, the theory is wrong is it not? The Bible tells you so.

Timeline Segment Summary: Time Block 4D

For the second half of the week of Daniel (1 260 days), and the start of Terror 3, see the Bible verses below:

* The End of the Prostitute Babylon city: Revelation 14:8, Revelation 17:16–17, Revelation 18
* Abomination of Desolation (Statue of the Eighth king, Little Horn): Daniel 12:11, Mark 13:14, Revelation 13:14–17
* Mark of the Beast: Revelation 13:16–18, Revelation 14:9–11

* The Elect 144 000 and any other followers of Christ subdued and conquered: Daniel 7:21 & 25, Revelation 12:17, Revelation 13:7–10 & 15

Time Block 4E

Terror 3 Continues—Massive Angelic War on Earth: Revelation 14:14-16, Revelation 15, Revelation 16

The Time Block Overview													
The End Begins	Rise of the Modern World	Jesus Revealed [Day of the LORD]		The Three Terrors					Jesus Returns [Day of the LORD]		1 000-Year Reign		Judgment [Day of the LORD] and New Creation
1	2		3		4				5		6		7
A	A	B	A	B	A	B	C	D	E	A	B	A	B	A	B

The Third Terror—Massive War & Seven Bowls of God's Wrath.

The Massive War and the Seven Bowls

There is a massive war coming, the like of which we have never experienced in the history of humanity; and it is coming to destroy the final Beast Kingdom after Time Block 4D and the Abomination of Desolation.

This war does not just involve mankind against mankind, but angels, demons, Beasts, and mankind against each other. It involves the Heavens and the Earth, and as a climax Jesus will return and take the victory.

One splendid prophecy from Isaiah 34 is a prophecy about this sort of event that is to befall everyone on Earth during the 30 days of Time Block

4E. We can say that the final portion of this prophecy has not been fulfilled as yet at the time of writing.

Here are verses 1–5:

> Come here and listen, O nations of the earth. Let the world and everything in it hear my words. For the Lord is enraged against the nations. His fury is against all their armies.
>
> He will completely destroy them, dooming them to slaughter. Their dead will be left unburied, and the stench of rotting bodies will fill the land. The mountains will flow with their blood.
>
> The heavens above will melt away and disappear like a rolled-up scroll. The stars will fall from the sky like withered leaves from a grapevine, or shriveled figs from a fig tree.
>
> And when my sword has finished its work in the heavens, it will fall upon Edom, the nation I have marked for destruction. NLT

This gives us a summary of the sort of battle to happen, and there is a blurring into the Day of the Lord coming up mentioned in Isaiah 34:4. Also, we see in Isaiah 34:5 God's sword being satiated in Heaven first, before coming down to analogous Edom—this shows the final and forever removal of all who are against God in Heaven.

In the end, if you continue to read Isaiah 34, 'Edom' becomes a precursor to the Lake of Fire described in Revelation 19:20 and Revelation 20:10 with eternal burning pitch and soils of sulfur. The fire will never be quenched.

There is one part of Revelation 12 that also seems to describe the mighty war involving Heaven, but in a different order—as afterwards it seems to reverse back to the start of the Terrors. See Revelation 12:7–8:

> Then there was war in heaven. Michael and his angels fought against the dragon and his angels. And the dragon lost the battle, and he and his angels were forced out of heaven. NLT

Perhaps the key here is the battle described in Heaven in Revelation 12 only occurs in Heaven. Whereas the mighty battle in Time Block 4E also involves the Earth.

The End of Terror Three

One of the difficulties I had understanding and discerning the end times was: where is the end of Terror Three? The Angels of Heaven in Revelation

Time Block 4E

8:13 declare there are three angels to blow trumpets to herald three Terrors (or woes). We clearly know two as Revelation 9:12 and Revelation 11:14 bookmark them for us. But where does it say, "the third Terror has passed"?

The hints we have for the third Terror are Revelations 11:14 where the third Terror (or "Woe") is coming quickly; and Revelation 12:12 where the loud voice from Heaven says "Woe to the Earth and the sea . . . "

The rest of Revelation 12 and 13 describe what I have in Time Blocks 4C and 4D. Therefore, the start of Terror Three is the Beast King taking full control in Time Block 4D, and culminates in true terror and woe of Time Block 4E.

So, where is the end of the third Terror or Woe?

There doesn't seem to be a mention like the ends of Terror One and Two, but surely it has to be after the Day of the Lord when Jesus returns with his tribulation saints and his angels, or at the start of the Millennial Reign of Christ (Time Block 6A) when everything is finished regarding Satan, Beast king, and Antichrist—for then, after Time Block 5A, there is a time of peaceful order and not terror or woe.

The Archangel Michael Rises

Archangel Michael rises for two crucial events: firstly, a messenger angel gives him the command to start the harvest of the Earth; secondly, he leads the final massive battle between the worldly Beast Kingdom (powered by Satan) and by the Heavenly realm (The Father).

The first harvest is the gathering of the Saints of the Tribulation. These must have come to Jesus throughout the Terrors etc. and refused the mark of the Beast Kingdom. It is important to note that this harvest is *not* the 144 000 elect. There is a clear distinction provided to grant us understanding, and you can find this in Revelation 14:1–5 and Revelation 15:1–4. Here are the important differences:

Revelation 14:1, 3:

> Then I saw the Lamb standing on Mount Zion, and with him were 144 000 who had his name and his Father's name written on their foreheads.
>
> This great choir sang a wonderful new song in front of the throne of God and before the four living beings and the twenty-four elders. No one could learn this song except the 144 000 who had been redeemed from the earth. NLT

Revelation 15: 2–3:

> I saw before me what seemed to be a glass sea mixed with fire. And on it stood all the people who had been victorious over the beast and his statue and the number representing his name. They were all holding harps that God had given them. And they were singing the song of Moses, the servant of God, and the song of the Lamb:
> "Great and marvelous are your works, O Lord God, the Almighty.
> Just and true are your ways, O King of the nations..."[NLT]

Did you notice the difference? One set of people sing a song no one but they can understand. The other set sing a song given by Moses and sung by you and me if we wish to.

So, the gathering of the Saints (new or old Christians that endured the hell of the Terrors) occurs *right at the start* of the seven bowls of wrath in Time Block 4E. If you carry on reading Revelation 15, you will agree, I'm sure. Whereas the 144 000 are gathered up to Jesus on his return in glory and power, and stand on Zion on the start of the second Day of the Lord in this study, right at the start of Time Block 5A. Here they sing that new song no one but they can learn.

In terms of prophecy separated by thousands of years, we have Malachi 3:1–2: Jesus tells us in Luke 7:26–27 that this is fulfilled in John the Baptist; but note that Jesus stops at the first sentence of Malachi 3:1.

The scripture then continues and deals with the Lord suddenly coming to his temple, and that there is a terrible time of cleansing. This portion does not seem to be fulfilled yet.

So, in terms of typical prophecy, Malachi 3:1–2 can also apply to Michael the Archangel messenger, preparing the way through a mighty battle and seven bowls of wrath for our Lord: Jesus. Here is the scripture for your discernment:

> "Behold, I send my messenger, and he will prepare the way before me. And the Lord whom you seek will suddenly come to his temple; and the messenger of the covenant in whom you delight, behold, he is coming, says the Lord of hosts. But who can endure the day of his coming, and who can stand when he appears? For he is like a refiner's fire and like fullers' soap." [ESV]

Have a read of Malachi 3:1–5 and decide for yourself, in the context of the Day of the Lord to come soon (in Time Block 5A); especially as Malachi states, "who can endure the day of his coming, who can stand when he appears?"

Time Block 4E

Harvesting the Earth—Or Post Tribulation Rapture

The two harvests of the Earth mentioned in Revelation 14:14–20 take some discerning. It took some revelation by the Holy Spirit for me to wake up to the fact that: one harvest is for the followers of God that endured (as described on page 91), and the other harvest is for those who reject and hate God.

Here are the two harvests:

> Then another angel came from the Temple and shouted to the one sitting on the cloud, "Swing the sickle, for the time of harvest has come; the crop on earth is ripe." So the one sitting on the cloud swung his sickle over the earth, and the whole earth was harvested.
>
> After that, another angel came from the Temple in heaven, and he also had a sharp sickle. Then another angel, who had power to destroy with fire, came from the altar. He shouted to the angel with the sharp sickle, "Swing your sickle now to gather the clusters of grapes from the vines of the earth, for they are ripe for judgment." So the angel swung his sickle over the earth and loaded the grapes into the great winepress of God's wrath. NLT

One of the clues for the different types of gathering is that the first harvest is of corn or wheat. Jesus tells his disciples that the followers of Jesus are like a crop of wheat, in both the parable of the sower (Mark 4:1–9) and when he tells them the crop is already ripe (John 4:34–37). We are the grain that is planted perishable, to become the imperishable.

The second harvest is of grapes. Grapes and wine are often related to wrath in the Bible, where the cup of God's wrath is drunk to the dregs. Joel 3:11–16 mentions the latter harvest, and here are verses 13–15:

> Put in the sickle, for the harvest is ripe. Go in, tread, for the winepress is full.
>
> The vats overflow, for their evil is great. Multitudes, multitudes, in the valley of decision!
>
> For the Day of the Lord is near in the valley of decision. The sun and the moon are darkened, and the stars withdraw their shining. ESV

With these passages, we can see that the first harvest is of the Tribulation Saints, that will become rulers with Christ in the 1 000 years during Time Block 6A coming up.

The second is quite a horrendous harvest of slaying and crushing, with descriptions of blood flowing to the height of horse's bridals—this slaying happens right as Jesus returns with his army. Hopefully, the amount of blood and gore described is poetic language used by John and not literal.

Why 30 Days for the Seven Bowls?

As mentioned before—why this mighty battle takes one Hebrew month to complete all comes down to Daniel and his week of years: a week of Hebrew years = 360 * 7 = 2 520 days. Now, Daniel 9:27 tells us in the New Living Translation Bible that:

> "The ruler will make a treaty with the people for a period of one set of seven, but after half this time, he will put an end to the sacrifices and offerings. And as a climax to all his terrible deeds, he will set up a sacrilegious object that causes desecration, until the fate decreed for this defiler is finally poured out on him." NLT

It is likely that at least three other periods in history have fulfilled this sacrilegious object in the temple (see also Daniel 11:31–34), but in a Typical Prophecy manner this will be the exact style of the final Beast King's desecration. Repetition like this appears to be a pattern for this sort of evil as it exerts its pride and power.

God's people are given a treaty (remember them having rest in the wilderness for 42 months or 1 260 days); then after half a week of years the Ruler sets up the statue. Half of 2 520 days is 1 260 days.

Daniel is also told the shattering of the Holy People will take Time, Times, and Half a Time (one Hebrew year, two Hebrew years, plus half a Hebrew year = 1 260 days). This is the war and persecution of the holy people (tribulation saints) of Time Block 4D on page 85, illuminated by Daniel 7:25:

> He shall speak words against the Most High and shall wear out the saints of the Most High, and shall think to change the times and the law; and they shall be given into his hand for a time, times, and half a time. ESV

Let's get back to the 30 days: Jesus points us to Daniel; when Daniel asks, "How will it all finally end?" he is told that "from the time the sacrifices are stopped and the Abomination of Desolation set up, there are 1 290 days." This means it all ends 1 290 days later, after 1 260 days of violent persecution. This gives us the 30 days for Michael rising, first harvest of the saints, the Seven Bowls of wrath and huge war.

To be honest, you could read the section from the New Living Translation out of context, as meaning 1 290 days between the end of sacrifices to the setting up of the statue. Which would mean the statue is set up right before the Day of the Lord. This cannot be correct, for a simple reason— how would that allow the statue to force everyone to worship the Beast and take the mark? I'm sure even I could last a day without buying or selling anything right? Hence, after the raising of the statue, there has to be a reasonable long period before the end comes. Daniel 7:25 tells us this period.

How about those blessed who endure to 1 335 days? Well, that's coming up in Time Block 5A + 5B. However, why it is 45 days later than the arrival of the Day of the Lord I couldn't say; no Holy Spirit guidance there, sorry! Maybe the Day of the Lord lasts for 45 mighty, holy, incredible days?

Timeline Segment Summary: Time Block 4E

For the scripture that deals with the great battle and the harvesting of the Earth, see the following passages to study:

* Terrible battle in Heaven and Earth before Jesus Returns: Isaiah 34:1–11, Zephaniah 1:14–18, Zephaniah 3:8, Joel 3:9–14, Mark 13:19–20
* Seven Bowls of wrath poured out during the battle: Revelation 16:1–16
* Defeat of the Little Horn: Daniel 7:26
* Archangel Michael leads the battle: Daniel 12:1–7, Malachi 3:1–2
* The separate gatherings:
  a. First the believers before the great battle: Daniel 12:1, 1 Thessalonians 4:15–16, Revelation 15:1–4, Revelation 14:14–16
  b. Then the 144 000 Israelite Elect as Jesus returns: 1 Thessalonians 4:17–18, Revelation 14:1–5
  c. More descriptions of gatherings and transformations: Isaiah 26:19–21, 1 Corinthians 15:50 – 57
* Do not worship the Beast, or accept that mark: Revelation 14:9–11

Time Block 5A

Jesus Returns—The Day of the Lord: Revelation 14:17-20, Revelation 16:17-21, Revelation 19

The Time Block Overview						
The End Begins	Rise of the Modern World	Jesus Revealed [Day of the LORD]	The Three Terrors	Jesus Returns [Day of the LORD]	1 000-Year Reign	Judgment [Day of the LORD] and New Creation
1	2	3	4	5	6	7
A	A | B	A | B	A | B | C | D | E	A | B	A | B	A | B

The Day of The Lord: Jesus and his Army Returns in Force.

This is not Judgment Day

No, this is not Judgment Day. For that, look at Time Block 7A coming up later, which is indeed Judgment Day, and the final Day of the Lord.

Although Revelation passages prior to this moment talk about the courts and the judgment seat, this day is more of an *enough is enough* judgment rebuke by almighty God. He proceeds to remove the source of evil and corruption in terms of both spiritual and earthly realm, and plants his feet on the ground to show humanity who God actually is, again.

Remember: before this the Abomination of Desolation, due to the Antichrist, was forcing people to worship the Beast as God and indeed they

Time Block 5A

were doing so. Here we see God returning in his physical presence as Jesus and setting all that straight.

Interestingly, Job declares this moment when his Redeemer will stand upon the earth (or dust) during one of Job's arguments with his friends, thousands and thousands of years before in Job 19:23–29. The Holy Spirit guided me here, especially with the end judgment. Here's what Job says:

> "Oh that my words were written! Oh that they were inscribed in a book!
>
> Oh that with an iron pen and lead they were engraved in the rock forever!
>
> For I know that my Redeemer lives, and at the last he will stand upon the earth.
>
> And after my skin has been thus destroyed, yet in my flesh I shall see God, whom I shall see for myself, and my eyes shall behold, and not another.
>
> My heart faints within me!"
>
> If you say, "How we will pursue him!" and, "The root of the matter is found in him," be afraid of the sword, for wrath brings the punishment of the sword, that you may know there is a judgment." ESV

So yes, there is a judgment called upon the inhabitants of the Earth and Heavens, but it isn't *the* final judgment.

This moment is also the well-known Second Coming of Christ. Remember that the first "Second Coming of Christ" in the Red Moon and Black Sun event is actually the revealing of Jesus in Time Block 3A, and cannot be the same, due to what happens before and after (revisit the Tables on pages 40 and 41). Here, in this Time Block, it is the second time he returns to *physically* stand on the planet and rule over the Earth.

When was the first time he stood physically on the Earth and walked amongst us? Time Block 1A, when he was born and ministered and served us.

This follows all scripture, in all relevant contexts. In the earlier Time Block 3A, Jesus is revealed to gather the Bride, but does not stand on the Earth. Instead he returns to his Father's house with his bride. I hope this clarifies the physical Second Coming of this Time Block, and the "Return and Revealing" of Time Block 3A. Confusion abounds about them being the same instance, and hopefully I have not confused it more.

Darkened Sun, Dark Moon

This is the other celestial sign discussed back in Time Block 3A and shown in the Tables on pages 40 and 41. No light from the sun, no light from the moon, no stars shining, or alternatively stars are falling. Yet there is a dawn spreading: a glorious army shining as they come in force, never seen before. Here is Joel 2:2 and 11:

> It is a day of darkness and gloom,
>   a day of thick clouds and deep blackness.
> Suddenly, like dawn spreading across the mountains,
>   a great and mighty army appears.
> Nothing like it has been seen before
>   or will ever be seen again . . .
> . . . The Lord is at the head of the column.
>   He leads them with a shout.
> This is his mighty army,
>   and they follow his orders.
> The day of the Lord is an awesome, terrible thing.
>   Who can possibly survive? NLT

Hopefully, the 144 000 special servants would have told the people of the Earth about this sign, so they know what to do. It is likely though, due to the nature of the times when this occurs, most peoples will refuse to repent.

God repeatedly uses this significant Day of the Lord sign in the Bible as a signpost for his wrath. For an instance that has already been fulfilled—Isaiah 13:9-10 prophesized about the original Babylon and the leader Cyrus that would ultimately free God's people back then.

Is it a Day? Maybe, Maybe Not—But Focus on the Message

The Bible tells us that a day is like a thousand years to the Lord, and a thousand years is like a day. For me, that clearly means God is not constrained by the spacetime he created. He is the potter, not the clay. For God to be constrained by spacetime is like a potter that made a vessel around himself, and then fired it in a kiln.

With this in mind, is the Day of the Lord an actual one-day period? Could it be 45 days long and therefore explain the "Blessed are those who endure to 1 335 days" after the Abomination of Desolation? Maybe. We could easily blend Time Block 5A and 5B together and it could equate to the Day of the Lord quite nicely. Study what is happening in both Time Blocks during those periods and decide for yourself.

I believe the Day of the Lord is the day he comes back with his army, and all the events described can be in one day or blended over the 45 days until Time Block 6A. When you read all that is happening, we should concentrate on the important message, rather than how long the Day of the Lord is.

So what is that message? That throughout the Bible we see God allows humanity and Satan to have their way, through free will—*up to a point*. At that point God comes back in force and gives people the option to come back to him, through his asking and their accepting of his invite. You see this so much in the Bible that you cannot miss it.

God allows us to play our games until he has to remind us who is Holy of Holy's, King of Kings and Lord of all. Then he opens his arms and says "come back children" and leaves us to decide.

This particular Day of The Lord is the biggest *enough is enough* in the history of the Earth and Heavens, due to Satan and humanity given totally free rein. God says this to the Beast, the Antichrist, the Foul Spirits, and to Satan, along with those humans that have fallen into the Beast's ways.

God punishes severely in this Time Block as a culmination of the Great Battle beforehand. This Time Block seems more destructive, more terrifying, and more horrendous than the actual Judgment Day of Time Block 7A, or even the last battle ever on Earth in Time Block 6B.

The Gathering of the 144 000

Here, as Jesus returns to end the mighty war of Time Block 4E, we see he gathers up and places those elected 144 000 Israelites on Zion with him, the Lamb of God. This is described in Revelation 14:1, 4:

> *The Lamb and the 144 000*
> Then I saw the Lamb standing on Mount Zion, and with him were 144 000 who had his name and his Father's name written on their foreheads . . .
> . . . They have kept themselves as pure as virgins, following the Lamb wherever he goes. They have been purchased from among the people on the earth as a special offering to God and to the Lamb. They have told no lies; they are without blame. NLT

Notice the final words above, and see Zephaniah 3:13 below:

> The remnant of Israel will do no wrong; they will never tell lies or deceive one another. They will eat and sleep in safety, and no one will make them afraid." NLT

They never tell lies and are blameless. These are a special offering to God as the first fruits of the harvests of peoples, and are destined to become something very special in the coming reign of Christ on Earth.

The Feast of Flesh

Unfortunately, the people that rage against God and Jerusalem as a huge rampant army get slain in one place, as per the second gathering we discussed at the end of Time Block 4E. This leads to the rather graphic and horrendous feast of flesh where The Word of God calls in the birds of the air to gorge themselves on the bodies.

Satan, The Beast, The False Prophet

Right at the end of the Day of the Lord, the Beast (Little Horn) is captured, as is the False Prophet (Antichrist) and these are thrown into the lake of fire—see Daniel 7:11:

> I continued to watch because I could hear the little horn's boastful speech. I kept watching until the fourth beast was killed and its body was destroyed by fire. NLT

Here they are destroyed eternally—that is; have eternal destruction played out.

Satan, however, is not thrown into the lake of fire. This is interesting as he actually still has a job to do for God whether he likes it, knows it, or not. For now, as his kingdom is destroyed forever, he is bound in the abyss for the coming Time Blocks of Jesus's reign. This abyss is likely to be the same abyss where the Angel of Death or Destroyer and his army came out of.

Note that no mention is made of what happens to the Abomination of Desolation; but then as this is just an animated statue, it has no importance. It was just a prop used by Satan, the Beast King, and the Antichrist to enforce their cruelty and fool the masses. It is a lifeless idol with no eternal soul to destroy. This is the ultimate mockery of lifeless idols. These have plagued mankind and God's people throughout the Old Testament, and the End Times. Often God would point out to people, through his prophets, how useless it was to make idols and then pray to them; God states he is the Living God who can really be trusted to protect and provide.

At the end, Satan finally made an idol that really appeared to have life, and the people had to worship it—importantly if they refused, they had to worship it by *force*. Note that the Holy and Righteous God never forces us to worship him. That's a free choice.

Ultimately, there is no salvation through worship of this Satan inspired statue, just as God repeatedly warns us.

The Wedding Feast

This is a bit of an odd one, as we always associate wedding feasts with much merriment. There could be much merriment of the wedding guests I suppose—but for those not invited; they get a whole world of upset. See Revelation 19:7-8:

> "Let us be glad and rejoice, and let us give honor to him.
>   For the time has come for the wedding feast of the Lamb, and his bride has prepared herself.
>   She has been given the finest of pure white linen to wear." For the fine linen represents the good deeds of God's holy people.^{NLT}

And then an angle declares in Revelation 19:17-18:

> Then I saw an angel standing in the sun, shouting to the vultures flying high in the sky: "Come! Gather together for the great banquet God has prepared. Come and eat the flesh of kings, generals, and strong warriors; of horses and their riders; and of all humanity, both free and slave, small and great." ^{NLT}

As we travel through the steps in the End Times wedding ceremony, this is the point where the happy couple, after a period of rest, should appear in fine display for all the guests to see and rejoice over. The happy couple being Jesus the Groom, and the Bride being all followers of Jesus, including the saints and followers that have come out of the Terrors; but in a rather ironic way the beasts of the air get their own special feast of flesh, and I would not call that rejoicing.

If we think of the intended view of the joyous wedding feast (i.e., not during the culmination of a mighty bloody battle) it might be more fitting for the Wedding Feast of Jesus and his Bride to be the golden age of the 1 000-year reign coming up in Time Block 5B. During that era following the Day of the Lord, Jesus's guests would have peace and merriment under the reign of their God on Earth, and could come and see the Bride and Groom on display in all their finery on Zion.

Timeline Segment Summary: Time Block 5A

There is much Biblical prophecy that deals with this well-known Day of the Lord. Have a look at the in-depth passages below for further study:

* Day of the Lord—darkened sun, dark moon: Joel 2:1–11, Joel 3:13–16, Amos 5:18–20, Zephaniah 1:14–18, Zechariah 14:6–7, Matthew 24:29–31, Mark 13:24–27, Jude 14–15, Revelation 17:14
* Jewish Wedding, Bride and Groom Revealed to All: Revelation 19:7–9
* The Beast Kingdom and Leaders are no more: Daniel 7:9–12, Revelation 19:19–20
* Jesus is Messiah—the mighty deliverer: Daniel 7:13–14, Psalm 97:1–9, Mark 14:61–62, Revelation 19:11–16
* Terrible Feast: Isaiah 66:15–16, Ezekiel 39:4, 17–20, Joel 3:13, Revelation 14:19–20, Revelation 19:15–21
* Culmination of the Day of the Lord: Isaiah 13:13, Isaiah 24:19–23, Ezekiel 38:17–23, Haggai 2:6–9, Revelation 11:15–19[1] Revelation 16:17–21
* The Elect stand with Jesus the Messiah: Revelation 14:1–5
* The beginnings of the transition to the Messiah's rule: Psalm 2, Malachi 3:3–5

---

1. Note: The New Living Translation Bible has a heading "The Seventh Trumpet Brings the Third Terror." However, as we have seen, the Third Terror begins when the Abomination of Desolation is set up. In the passages given we can clearly see it is the Victory of Christ on the Day of the Lord and the start of His eternal kingdom.

Time Block 5B

The 44 Day Transition—Or the Day of the Lord Continues: Revelation 20:1-6

The Time Block Overview							
The End Begins	Rise of the Modern World	Jesus Revealed [Day of the LORD]	The Three Terrors			Jesus Returns [Day of the LORD]	1 000-Year Reign	Judgment [Day of the LORD] and New Creation
1	2	3	4			5	6	7
A	A | B	A | B	A | B | C | D | E			A | B	A | B	A | B

The Day of The Lord: Events Continue – The Transition.

Satan is Taken Out of the Equation

This current Time Block 5B is the capture of Satan and the revealing of the First Resurrection: people who receive the very first new bodies, based on the Lamb of God Jesus, who is the New Adam.

With the Beast and Antichrist defeated by Jesus and his army, with Archangel Michael as the Prince under the King of Kings, we see Satan now taken and chained as a prisoner of war for 1 000 years. He is thrown into The Bottomless Pit or Abyss which is then closed and locked for a purpose. The purpose? So that he could not deceive the nations anymore until his prison sentence is complete (see Revelation 20:1-3).

Don't miss this important point: From Adam in the Book of Genesis to this Christ Returning Day of The Lord, Satan has constantly deceived, whispered, and attacked us. See what he does to the man Job when given *almost* free rein in the Book of Job. Not to mention the sort of global empire he powers when allowed to by God in Time Blocks 4C, 4D and 4E.

Now, in Time Block 5B and Time Block 6A he has *absolutely no influence on humanity.* Why? Because coming up is the final chance of humanity's residual souls to accept Jesus, or reject Jesus. I believe (my thoughts, not Holy Spirit inspired) God wants them to be clear-headed, without Satan's influence, to make their choice with just pure human logic and mind. Even now, right near the end, God is still offering a way out of damnation.

I can say with 100 percent certainty that no one today can imagine what it would be like to be free of Satan's influence, whispers, and deception. It runs so deep in our lives and cultures around the world. He is a defeated enemy but relentless in his goal to seemingly bring us all to destruction with himself. Satan even tried to tempt Jesus, his God and creator! To be free of this constant source of subversion would be a great release for humanity, would it not?

Beast Kingdom Leaders and Heavenly Associates (Fallen Angels) Imprisoned

From Isaiah 24:21–22 (which is without doubt part of the end of the Day of the Lord) and Daniel 7:12, we find that those responsible for the Beast Kingdom and enforcing its authority are imprisoned. Maybe for the 1 000 years before Judgment Day? Here is the Isaiah passage:

> On that day the Lord will punish the host of heaven, in heaven, and the kings of the earth, on the earth. They will be gathered together as prisoners in a pit; they will be shut up in a prison, and after many days they will be punished. ESV

In some Bible translations, Daniel declares they have their dominion taken for a season and a time, and although I understand the notion of how long a "time" is (one Hebrew year), I don't know about a "season." Maybe a quarter of a Hebrew year? Is it important? They are imprisoned and out of the way.

Time Block 5B

The First Resurrection

The most important life goal you should have is to become one of the First Resurrected, if you still can.

To be one of these is a great blessing, as you get to be with Jesus and reign with him in a righteous and holy way, the like of which has never been seen on Earth, especially in these modern times.

To become a First Resurrected is to be completely, wholeheartedly, accepted by God in Jesus and to be adopted forever into his household. You will no longer need to suffer, worry, hunger, thirst, or cry out for justice. You will be kind authority to the world, and serve Jesus directly, personally, as he loves you completely.

If that is not enough, then consider the truth that by being a First Resurrected your new body will be based on the sinless New Adam of Christ. The benefits and outcome of this fact includes the ability to do what Jesus could do after his resurrection recorded for us in the book of Luke chapter 24. Take a read of that entire chapter. Teleportation anyone? Yes please!

To see who these First Resurrected are, here is what God's word says in Revelation 20:4-5:

> Then I saw thrones, and the people sitting on them had been given the authority to judge. And I saw the souls of those who had been beheaded for their testimony about Jesus and for proclaiming the word of God. They had not worshiped the beast or his statue, nor accepted his mark on their foreheads or their hands. They all came to life again, and they reigned with Christ for a thousand years.
>
> This is the first resurrection. (The rest of the dead did not come back to life until the thousand years had ended.)[NLT]

Who are they? The first set of people mentioned in Revelation 20:4 must be the gathered Bride from Time Block 3A during the rapture event, or those that died in Christ beforehand. These are given authority by Jesus (Revelation 2:10-11, Revelation 2:26-28, Revelation 3:11-12, Revelation 3:19-21), and they now serve Jesus in the Messianic Temple.

However, the honor to sit as Judge, or on Jesus's Throne, is a reward for those Christians who stay steadfast against all sort of false teachings and comfortable "don't rock the boat" faith, as explained in Revelation 2 and 3. Jesus holds his Bride accountable to act accordingly as warned in those chapters, so that they don't stray and do indeed get their reward.

With that in mind, here is an interesting point to remember: there is no *salvation* through works, or what you do, or how good you think you are. Instead, *after* salvation through grace and having your name written in the Book of Life, the way you act as a Christian seems to define the extra rewards you receive in Heaven. Paul in 2 Corinthians 5:6–10 declares this fact, and indeed the apostle James makes a point of stating that faith without works is a dead faith. So first comes Salvation through grace, then comes works showing the faith is alive. Here is a snippet of James 2:14–26:

> What good is it, dear brothers and sisters, if you say you have faith but don't show it by your actions? Can that kind of faith save anyone? Suppose you see a brother or sister who has no food or clothing, and you say, "Good-bye and have a good day; stay warm and eat well"—but then you don't give that person any food or clothing. What good does that do?
>
> So you see, faith by itself isn't enough. Unless it produces good deeds, it is dead and useless. NLT

Back to the First Resurrected: the next set of people mention in Revelation 20:4 encapsulates a host of believers. These are the martyred for the sake of Christ, including those in all the Terrors, and those that truly suffered horrors and were killed because they did not worship the Beast nor accept its mark: the Tribulation Saints and any that accept Christ after Time Block 3A.

As per Revelation 5:10:

> And you have caused them to become a Kingdom of priests for our God. And they will reign on the earth. NLT

These chosen people will be priest of, and reign with, Jesus for a thousand years while the rest of the dead wait. Also, the second death has no hold over these First Resurrection people. What is the second death? We'll come to that in Time Block 7A and 7B.

Note: we also have Psalm 102:12–22 again (it was right at the start in Time Block 1A), written for future generations, so that a people not yet born (or in some translations, not yet created) will praise the Lord. Now, this prophecy can be reapplied to the people subdued and imprisoned by the Beast Kingdom, along with what is coming up; multitudes and kingdoms will come up to Jerusalem to worship the Lord in Time Block 6A.

Time Block 5B

Language Purified

In this Time Block 5B, we see a hint of something that reverses what happened in the Old Testament story of the Tower of Babel (Genesis 11:1–8). In that old, old message, God in Three mixed up languages so that we could not all work together against him and rebel against his command to spread out and fill the Earth. After all, God wanted his people to spread across the world, not sit dormant and stagnate in Babel.

But now, after the triumphant return of Jesus in the Day of the Lord, we see something odd: the purification of speech so that humanity can worship the Lord with *one name*—see Zephaniah 3:9:

> "For at that time I will change the speech of the peoples to a pure speech, that all of them may call upon the name of the Lord and serve him with one accord." ᴱˢⱽ

And Zechariah 14:9:

> And the Lord will be king over all the earth. On that day the Lord will be one and his name one. ᴱˢⱽ

Will that name be Jesus? Unlikely, as that is not his Hebrew name. It doesn't matter what name God chooses for us to all praise him as one, as we'll all know it. Furthermore, we will be able to say it globally without confusion.

Again, there will be no distraction caused by Satan's influence. Everyone left on Earth will know the name of God and will be able to praise him as one, if they choose. No different religions. No confusion over who God is. He is sat right there on his throne on Earth, with one name.

Life During the Transition, and After the Day of the Lord

There are two distinct ways of being after the Day of the Lord, when Jesus is now in his Messianic Temple. One is to follow him and take refuge in him. The other is to go against him and face stern rulings. I touch on this more in Time Block 6A during the 1 000-year reign of Christ. The passage that follows describes this decidedly polarized choice:

Psalm 2:10–12:

> Now then, you kings, act wisely!
>   Be warned, you rulers of the earth!

> Serve the Lord with reverent fear, and rejoice with trembling.
> Submit to God's royal son, or he will become angry, and you will be destroyed in the midst of all your activities—for his anger flares up in an instant.
> But what joy for all who take refuge in him! ᴺᴸᵀ

The good news is there is no longer any deceiving influence of Satan to muddy the waters. The peoples of this time can, with clear minds, submit to Jesus as King and have joy (Psalm 2:12 last sentence and Revelation 7:16-17). But reject him, and what terrible times you bring on yourself—ruled by a rod of iron by Jesus and the First Resurrected creation.

Timeline Segment Summary: Time Block 5B

Here are the in-depth study verses that deal with this transitional phase, and the beginning of the Millennial Reign of Christ on Earth. Also note that this seemingly lasts 45 days after the moment Jesus returns to Earth in force, so that the special blessing occurs as per Daniel 12:12.

* First Resurrected: Philippians 3:20-21, 1 Corinthians 15:20-23, Revelation 5:9-10, Revelation 20:4-6
* Satan no longer influences mankind: Revelation 20:1-3
* Start of the 1 000-year reign of Jesus the Messiah: Psalm 47, Psalm 98, Psalm 102: 12-22, Daniel 7:13-14, Zechariah 2:1-5 & 10-13, Micah 5:2-5 (First Sentence)
* Language becomes purified: Zephaniah 3:9-13, Zechariah 14:9
* Authority granted by Jesus to rule with him: Revelation 2:26-28
* A blessing at 1335 days since the Abomination of Desolation: Daniel 12:12
* The 144 000 remnant Elect have a special mention: Zephaniah 3:12-13, Revelation 14:4-5, Micah 5:7-15

Time Block 6A

The 1 000 Year Reign of Christ on Earth: Revelation 20:4-6

The Time Block Overview							
The End Begins	Rise of the Modern World	Jesus Revealed [Day of the LORD]	The Three Terrors	Jesus Returns [Day of the LORD]	1 000- Year Reign	Judgment [Day of the LORD] and New Creation	
1	2	3	4	5	6	7	
A	A	B	A	B	A	B	C	D	E	A	B	A	B	A	B

Millennial Reign of Christ
Jesus in his Temple

Jesus Christ on Earth in Jerusalem

Revelation 14:1 states clearly that Jesus physically comes back to stand on Earth, and after the Day of the Lord and its transition period, we begin the 1 000 years of his reign as Messiah.

When I was a child I thought Judgment Day was all we got—then into heaven or hell. However, this is clearly not the case. Once you understand this, the rest of the Bible opens up a wealth of other related passages for Time Block 6A. Here is Zephaniah 3:15, 17:

> For the Lord will remove his hand of judgment and will disperse the armies of your enemy.
> And the Lord himself, the King of Israel, will live among you!

> At last your troubles will be over, and you will never again fear disaster...
>
> ...For the Lord your God is living among you. He is a mighty savior.
>
> He will take delight in you with gladness. With his love, he will calm all your fears.
>
> He will rejoice over you with joyful songs." ᴺᴸᵀ

But there is also a flip side to the Messiah living on Earth, as we read in Psalm 2:7–10. Jesus now rules with a rod of iron until all his enemies are under him. This is no longer the easy choice we have prior to Time Block 3A, to accept the gift of grace. Here in the 1 000 years, Jesus is more like a stern parent teaching wayward and dangerous children how to behave; as well as blessing and helping and protecting those that accept him.

Of course, people still have their own minds to make up, and this process of the 1 000 years does a good job of sorting out who is to be saved through rule and who will rebel and join with Satan when he is allowed out of the pit later. This may lead people to sit here in our comfortable lives and declare that Jesus acts like a dictator, but he is not a fallen person like us. Therefore, when Jesus rules with a rod of iron you know, and can have confidence, that it will be completely morally correct, completely right and just and there will be no hint of corruption, decadence or greed that befalls all human dictatorships. The closest analogy I can think of is a Righteous, Kind Monarchy of total power and dominion with zero corruption and favoritism.

Also, remember that there is no Satan during this period. He is locked away so he cannot give influence or power to anyone at all. So, imagine a Benevolent Monarchy (as my pastor was taught) leading a world population who were prone to murder, demon worship, debauchery, and moral decadence. Now they have a kind but stern King and are left to make up their own mind as to whether they accept Jesus or not, without the whispering or lies from Satan. It will make a huge difference to the way this world will be—but the concept is so alien for us to relate to as we are not free of today's corruption.

Time Block 6A

The Reinstatement of a Temple

There will be a requirement to go to Jerusalem at appointed times and festivals. It is clear in many Bible passages everyone will be called to kneel before the Son of God and declare him King of All.

As discussed previously (page 76), there has to be a Temple related to Jesus and his throne on Earth for this 1 000 years. If you recall the First Resurrection on page 105, these glorified people are to be *priests* of God and Jesus, as per Revelation 20:6:

> Blessed and holy is the one who shares in the first resurrection! Over such the second death has no power, but they will be priests of God and of Christ, and they will reign with him for a thousand years. ᴱˢⱽ

Also, Revelation 7:15 shows these people are to be servants of him who sits on the Throne in his temple. I have no doubt that Jesus will be in a physical third temple in Jerusalem, ministered by his servants and Priests along with the 144 000 elect.

For all those who wish to believe this has to be the final Heaven in the New Jerusalem, this cannot be so, for Revelation 21:22 clearly states there is *no* temple in the New Jerusalem that comes down from Heaven, for the Lord God and the Lamb *are* its temple.

One interesting Prophet in the Bible is Ezekiel, who saw amazing visions similar to John with regards Heaven, the angels and the One seated on the throne. Ezekiel wrote about a glorious new temple, in which the Lord himself comes and resides. This is in Ezekiel chapters 40–48 if you wish to read the design and purpose of this Law based temple; and here is where the trouble begins.

Recall at the start of this study, I said that one of my criteria was to be led by the Holy Spirit and try not to be conformed to what I know or have read before? Well, the Holy Spirit led me to this temple and the typical prophecy it contains, closely mirroring the new Heaven and Earth of Revelation 22. When you read Ezekiel 47, and indeed Zechariah 14:8–9, there is a river flowing out from beneath the temple; this river purifies the Dead Sea and produces fruit trees on each side that resemble the heavenly trees of Revelation 22. So, what is the troublesome issue?

It all came to a head for me with the sanity check pass through that I performed with my pastor. Simply put, Ezekiel's temple and the animal sacrifice system it contains seems to nullify Christ's sacrifice for us; once again we are back to animal sacrifices, clean and unclean, circumcised and uncircumcised, Israelis or Foreigners.

Remember, the only atonement and redemption (salvation) is through Jesus and his perfect sacrifice for us. So there is a potential contradiction on this side of the Day of the Lord, where we live today.

We know this Ezekiel Temple has not been built yet (the last one did not fit this description), and we know it will be desecrated by the Abomination of Desolation, before finally coming into play during the 1 000-year period when Jesus the King rules the peoples of the Earth.

Isaiah 66:20-21 also hints that there are priests and Levites in the 1 000-year period similar to the old sort that used to tend to the Jerusalem temples before AD 70:

> And they shall bring all your brothers from all the nations as an offering to the Lord, on horses and in chariots and in litters and on mules and on dromedaries, to my holy mountain Jerusalem, says the Lord, just as the Israelites bring their grain offering in a clean vessel to the house of the Lord. And some of them also I will take for priests and for Levites, says the Lord. ᴱˢⱽ

All this causes confusion—after all, the old Law was fulfilled in Christ and his sacrifice. So, why bring it back? A possible answer is a sort of punishment—there is a hint in Zechariah 14:16-21. Here is verse 16:

> Then everyone who survives of all the nations that have come against Jerusalem shall go up year after year to worship the King, the Lord of hosts, and to keep the Feast of Booths. ᴱˢⱽ

There is another hint too in Colossians 2:16-17 where Paul is reminding people that Christ is all you need, but he says "The Law and traditions are shadows of the things to come (but the substance, the body, belongs to Christ)." He also states that Christians are "circumcised by and of Christ."

So that tells us something about the future shown in Ezekiel 47, and perhaps clears up some of the contradictions: all Christians will become the New Adam type of creation, and so are "clean," "circumcised of the heart" and saved. We are also told Christians are grafted into God's Chosen people; the Israelites.

In summary here are the points I do know:

* There is a physical temple existing during and after the Beast Kingdom. After the defeat of the Beasts, Jesus our Lord sits within and is ministered by the Bride, the Elect and the Tribulation Saints, who also

Time Block 6A

share the authority. This could be the fulfillment of Isaiah 66:21, and definitely Revelation 7:15 and Revelation 20:6.

* Everyone will come to this temple as required.

* If you have accepted Christ as your savior and repented of your sins, *you are forgiven eternally.* Therefore the 1 000-year temple requirements *do not relate to you except for sharing the authority of Christ* who sits on the throne. You are no longer a fallen human, but part of the First Resurrection with the New Adam bodies given by Christ who transformed us. For proof of this, Hebrews 10:18 says:

   "And when sins have been forgiven, there is no need to offer any more sacrifices." NLT

* Some forms of Judaism declares this Ezekiel Temple to be the Third Temple fulfilled prior to, or during the Messianic Age.[1] Are these rejecting Christ? And therefore putting themselves under a new law of sacrifice that does nothing but subdue?

Although I firmly believe the Holy Spirit led me to connect the Ezekiel Temple to the 1 000-year period, I have no further guidance I can offer. What I can say is that it will all be very clear in the Millennial Reign of Christ!

The 144 000 Elect, Saints and More

During the Messianic Age, God now gives the chosen special offering (who kept themselves pure and never told lies) an important task to do in this 1 000-year reign: they become mighty servants, placed amongst the nations to destroy all pagan worship and evil doers as described in Micah 5:7–15. Here is what Micah 5:7–8 says:

> Then the remnant left in Israel will take their place among the nations.
> They will be like dew sent by the Lord or like rain falling on the grass, which no one can hold back and no one can restrain.
> The remnant left in Israel will take their place among the nations.

---

1. Wikipedia, *Third Temple*

> They will be like a lion among the animals of the forest, like a strong young lion among flocks of sheep and goats, pouncing and tearing as they go with no rescuer in sight. ^{NLT}

In addition, the ones who endured the Beast also have a similar part to play. These also have authority over the people of the Earth to rule with holy and blameless strength. See Revelation 2:26-28:

> The one who conquers and who keeps my works until the end, to him I will give authority over the nations, and he will rule them with a rod of iron, as when earthen pots are broken in pieces, even as I myself have received authority from my Father. And I will give him the morning star. ^{ESV}

The human population left on Earth that need this sort of strength and severity aimed against them are not poor, lowly people oppressed by some harsh dictator. Remember the demon worshipping, murdering, thefts and sexual immorality they were doing in Revelation 9? And then later they join up with the Beast to fight against God's army in the mighty war before the Day of the Lord.

Jesus will sit in Jerusalem as the King of Kings over all the nations, and he will have many appointed servants to do his work. All this is for one purpose—to subdue all worldly authority and bring it under God's Messiah Jesus, and to provide the final choice and sorting.

Also recall what happens to all the other Israelites who were not the chosen Elect 144 000. To remind you, Romans 11:25-27 has Paul telling us *all* Israel will be saved when the Deliverer comes from Zion. This deliverer is the Messiah Jesus, now in the Temple on Zion, teaching and being God on Earth from his temple.

Sheep and Goats—Salvation through Good Works?

Before we delve into this portion of Jesus's reign on Earth, which is towards the end of the period of 1 000 years, we have to state one truth as bedrock: there is no salvation given to you or anyone through the "good works" that you or anyone have done, or will do. Even if you know who Christ is, or even if you do not.

Paul tells us this in Titus 3:3-5, and this message is clearly repeated throughout the Bible. Only God gives salvation through His good pleasure, whether we have done good or not. Simply put, good works bears no relation to you receiving salvation from God. God didn't come to save the righteous remember! He came to save all of us, if you recall the King sending out invites to all and sundry on page 34.

Paul describes in Romans 2:12-16 that God's law is written on the hearts of everyone, and people demonstrate this by knowing they are doing wrong or right. God put his moral code on us, and we all know it.

So, to help with the 'Sheep and Goats' parable and Jesus sorting the nations, let me give you an illustration provided to me by the Holy Spirit.

Imagine there is a massive war happening, like World War 1. God conscripts some of us to fight under his command against the enemy, after some basic training. These are people like the apostles. They were ordered by God to join the fight, even though they may not have known him.

God also glued a poster of his call to fight against the enemy on the walls of our hearts (as per Romans 2:12-16), and the poster shows his moral law and very nature to be observed. It does not say "I need you" with a picture of a man pointing out. It says "accept the call to fight", with his arms welcoming you.

Most people just walk by that poster, look at it and ignore it, or reject it. Some even join the enemy! But there are others convicted to join up, volunteer and fight alongside those conscripted—all in the same army, fighting the same enemy, under the same commander. There is no-one that has missed that poster, for God glued it on the walls of *all* hearts.

Now, back to the Sheep and Goats parable. Read all of the parable in Matthew 25:31-46 before we continue.

During the reign of Jesus in his temple, all the nations will come to him and he will separate them out as either blessed or damned. Whether these people unknowingly accepted Christ in their hearts (as Christ fulfils God's law) or rejected him can be seen in what Jesus the King says to them.

The people who served and helped those that needed assistance, actually served Christ as he states "And the King will say, 'I tell you the truth, when you did it to one of the least of these my brothers and sisters, you were doing it to me!'"[NLT] They have accepted God in their hearts and they serve the King.

The people who selfishly ignored all needs and suffering before them are the ones that walk away from that poster on their hearts and reject God's nature and calling. These get the ticket to the Eternal Fire.

In conclusion, Jesus performs some physical sorting of peoples at this time in his reign, with them in front of him and being surprised that they got a blessing, or a curse. It is important to see *who* gives that blessing to eternal life, or salvation: Jesus commands them to 'come and inherit' those blessed by the Father. Again, their works did not save them—Jesus saved them due to the Father because they answered the call of the poster on their hearts—(it is at this point I should inform you that there is a bit of a division in the church about this last notion. Some Christians believe answering the call comes under 'works' and therefore cannot be part of receiving salvation. These ideas form an immense theological study that goes back thousands of years, and is not part of this book).

The nations the Sheep and Goats parable applies to are not the followers and accepters of Jesus, as there is no need for them to be sorted into sheep and goats – they are already a First Resurrected as discussed previously, or have accepted Jesus and repented due to teachings during this time, and so are already written into the Book of Life for later. So, these people from the nations must be those that do not know Jesus, and are required to come and meet him, in person, for the first time. Some of them may be from the remains of the Beast Kingdom brutality.

These people have also lived their lives without the influence of Satan, as he was put away for this period until the end of the 1 000 years.

What we see now, before Jesus, is our basic human nature divided into two kinds: those with a heart to serve the King, and those that want nothing to do with serving anyone. Unfortunately, when they are standing before the King it is too late to repent for any actions, as the sorting happens as they stand there; and from what we understand from the parable, they are all confused anyway.

Terrible Flesh Eating Madness Disease?

For those that fight against God or refuse to go up to him—and perhaps still wish for the destroyed Beast Kingdom (for undoubtedly there will be those that gained greatly in it)—there is a famine and plague sent. Here is Zechariah 14:12–13 as an example:

> And the Lord will send a plague on all the nations that fought against Jerusalem. Their people will become like walking corpses, their flesh rotting away. Their eyes will rot in their sockets, and their tongues will rot in their mouths. On that day they will be terrified, stricken by the Lord with great panic. They will fight their neighbors hand to hand. NLT

Time Block 6A

Lo and behold that sounds pretty horrendous; almost like the crazed infected of the British film "28 Days Later" mixed with flesh rotting like a zombie. You'll also discover in scripture the horses and mules and all other animals in the enemy camp will catch this disease too.

What is happening here? Well, even after the terrible and mighty Day of the Lord in Time Block 5A, and the removal of Satan's influence, there still seems to be some rebellion. There are still armies coming up against Jerusalem and Christ seated on his throne; but these attackers are doomed to this terrible zombie disease, and Isaiah 66:24 seems to provide more scriptural evidence of this.

Timeline Segment Summary: Time Block 6A

There is much the Bible says about Jesus reigning on Earth as the Messiah for the 1 000 years. Indeed, some of the Jewish people were convinced that when Jesus came the first time, he was going to start this reign on Earth and crush the Roman oppressors way back in this study's Time Block 1A.

Here are some important verses to look at for a deeper study:

* Summary of the 1 000-year Messiah Rule: Isaiah 11:4-16, Isaiah 60, Isaiah 61, Isaiah 65:18-25, Micah 4:1-8, Matthew 25:31-46
* Priests of God and Christ in the Temple: Revelation 2:26-28, Revelation 3:20-21, Revelation 5:9-10, Revelation 7:14-15, Revelation 20:6
* Peace for those that accept The Messiah Jesus: Psalm 23:1-5, Isaiah 2:1-4, Isaiah 9:7, Isaiah 12, Ezekiel 34:11-15, Zephaniah 3:10-20, Habakkuk 2:20
* Terrible times for those that fight against Jesus: Psalm 2, Zechariah 14:12-19, Isaiah 49:25-26, Isaiah 66:24
* All shall come and honor God: Psalm 22:27-31, Psalm 99:1-5, Isaiah 66:18-21, Daniel 7:27, Jeremiah 3:15-18, Hosea 3:5
* Temple worship and sacrifice, during Jesus's reign as Messiah:

    a. Examples of the Temple worship for those who do not accept Jesus: Ezekiel 40:38-46, Ezekiel 43:7-12, 18-27, Ezekiel 45:21-25
    b. But not for those who are Christ's: Hebrews 9:11-28, Hebrews 10:11-18

For in-depth and splendid study of this Ezekiel Temple in the Bible, and the issues this brings for Christianity, see David Guzik's Enduring Word webpage:

https://enduringword.com/bible-commentary/ezekiel-chapter-40/

TIME BLOCK 6B

Satan Released to Gather Followers. Instant Defeat: Revelation 20:7-10

The Time Block Overview														
The End Begins	Rise of the Modern World		Jesus Revealed [Day of the LORD]		The Three Terrors				Jesus Returns [Day of the LORD]		1 000-Year Reign		Judgment [Day of the LORD] and New Creation	
1	2		3		4				5		6		7	
A	A	B	A	B	A	B	C	D	E	A	B	A	B	A	B

The Final Non-Battle: Satan and his Followers Defeated

Amazing Non-Battle

At the end of his 1 000-year prison term chained in the pit, Satan is released. He then, without any care or love, gathers up the nations and followers that reject Jesus as Lord, by *deceiving* them! Does that sound fair? No, of course not. He knows he is a defeated enemy, so in a final act of cruelty he will drag down whoever he can, using deception, into the lake of fire reserved for him and his angels.

You only have to look at the way the internet and social media derailed the Western world by deception through self-serving lies, to see how easy it would be for Satan to do this to a population unsure about the kind but strong God in Jerusalem, ruling righteously.

The Bible doesn't give a clear idea of how long this period of gathering is. There is a vast army to muster and form up towards Jerusalem, where Jesus is waiting for them. How long does it take Satan to do this? I don't know.

What is clear is that the vast army comes to war against Christ; and with one word He defeats the entire army, plus the mighty cherub Satan, instantly. No battle, just a word and fire is brought into their midst. Ezekiel describes this Ezekiel 28:13–19. Here are verses 17–19:

> Your heart was filled with pride because of all your beauty.
> Your wisdom was corrupted by your love of splendor.
> So I threw you to the ground and exposed you to the curious gaze of kings.
> You defiled your sanctuaries with your many sins and your dishonest trade.
> So I brought fire out from within you, and it consumed you.
> I reduced you to ashes on the ground in the sight of all who were watching.
> All who knew you are appalled at your fate.
> You have come to a terrible end, and you will exist no more.
> NLT

And note Revelation 20:9:

> And I saw them as they went up on the broad plain of the earth and surrounded God's people and the beloved city. But fire from heaven came down on the attacking armies and consumed them.
> NLT

Ezekiel 28:11–19 starts out with a "Lament for the King of Tyre," but this ends up being so clearly about Satan: we know he was in the Garden of Eden, he is also a cherub, a mighty angel. Therefore, it takes little Holy Spirit inspiration to see of whom this lament speaks.[1]

With Satan joining the Beast and Antichrist in the Lake of Fire, the end has come for our entire spacetime bubble.

---

1. Take note that some translations are conflicting – Expanded Bible, Names of God Bible and Revised Standard Version are examples of this. Read and discern for yourself.

Time Block 6B

Timeline Segment Summary: Time Block 6B

See below for the limited study of this hardly mentioned battle (see the difference in amount of scripture!):

* People and Nations deceived to fight Jesus: Ezekiel 38:1–16, Revelation 20:7–8
* God's lament for his mighty guardian cherub Satan: Ezekiel 28:13–19
* Jesus defeats the final rejection with a word: Revelation 20:9–10

Time Block 7A

The Judgment of All—The Final Day of the Lord: Revelation 20:11–15

The Time Block Overview												
The End Begins	Rise of the Modern World	Jesus Revealed [Day of the LORD]		The Three Terrors				Jesus Returns [Day of the LORD]		1 000 Year Reign		Judgment [Day of the LORD] and New Creation
1	2	3		4				5		6		7
A	A	A	B	A	B	C	D	E	A	B	A	B	A	B

The End—The Final Day of the Lord.

Judgment Day—The Books are Opened.

The End! This *is* Judgment Day

Here is the moment we all stand before God and get into the New Heavens, New Earth, and New Jerusalem—or not. It is the culmination of the journey from Adam and Eve's fall in the Garden of Eden, and thousands upon thousands of years of God's plan to bring us back to live with him fully.

This truly is The End, with the subsequent eternity of Time Block 7B being an epilogue to the End Times.

Time Block 7A

Goodbye Spacetime

For all those who may have missed it: here is the total end to not only the world, but the very fabric of spacetime itself! God never intended this creation to last forever, and the Bible tells us this in Psalm 102:25–27:

> Of old you laid the foundation of the earth, and the heavens are the work of your hands. They will perish, but you will remain; they will all wear out like a garment. You will change them like a robe, and they will pass away but you are the same, and your years have no end. ESV

Think about what this means—*instant death* for every single creature alive in this Universe. You cannot physically exist without the basic atomic structures required to keep you together! That puts quite a kibosh on reincarnation too, for the Father has told us that there is no going back to this universe, but onwards once and for all into a new one with him.

This is the moment when *all souls* find themselves without the old Adam (Mankind) based body. So, what body do they have?

Everyone Gets a New Eternal Body

Like the people of the First Resurrection in Time Block 5B, everyone else now receives a New Adam (Son of God, Son of Man) based body. As John tells us in Revelation 20:5, after the 1000 years have ended the rest of the dead come to life. This would be the subsequent resurrection.

Jesus is the first born of the new creation; the New Adam, born of Spirit and Flesh. This means he is the sinless pattern that all our new bodies will be based on.

Interestingly, when Jesus died, the Father accepted the body Jesus used here on Earth as his new glorified body. It was without sin and was shown to be able to withstand temptation. That is why there is no body in the tomb at Easter. Jesus has been resurrected to eternal life, and on this notion hangs the whole of Christianity.

So, at last, we can be born of the Spirit into bodies that are incorruptible by that original Adam DNA strain of old! That ancient flesh pattern that Satan has had a good smirk with for thousands and thousands of years, and billions of suffering souls. All of us have new eternal bodies.

Jesus talks about resurrection in Mark 12:24-25:

> Jesus replied, "Your mistake is that you don't know the Scriptures, and you don't know the power of God. For when the dead rise, they will neither marry nor be given in marriage. In this respect they will be like the angels in heaven." ᴺᴸᵀ

With these new eternal bodies, we will eat, drink, feel emotion as it is supposed to be felt and be able to stand in the presence of God as holy.

Read what Jesus did with the Eternal body in Luke 24:36-43. Not only did Jesus come and go as he pleased (like manifesting himself into our space-time from the Heavenly realm) but also ate with his disciples and proved he was a real person: alive, physical, and not a ghost.

There is a terrible flip side to this: those who damn themselves to judgment and destruction are also likely to have the same eternal bodies. In Revelation 20:12-13, everywhere gives up its dead so they stand before the Throne, *after* our spacetime has been melted and gone. The imagery is of people standing in bodies, not disembodied souls (see Revelation 6:9-11 for an example of disembodied souls, as they are prior to the First Resurrection). Hence, the unfortunate nature of the ones who *reject* the grace of salvation with their indestructible new bodies: they are eternally in the lake of fire, or the outer darkness (wailing and gnashing of teeth). Neither are pleasant and the former is definitely eternal. I have no idea if the Outer Darkness is also eternally inescapable. We look at these two endings in the Time Block 7B chapter to follow.

The Parable of the Wedding Feast Ends

Here we see the conclusion of the very long thread of Matthew 22:1-14, with verses 11-14:

> "But when the king came in to look at the guests, he saw there a man who had no wedding garment. And he said to him, 'Friend, how did you get in here without a wedding garment?' And he was speechless. Then the king said to the attendants, 'Bind him hand and foot and cast him into the outer darkness. In that place there will be weeping and gnashing of teeth.' For many are called, but few are chosen." ᴱˢⱽ

The King comes to see the banquet of wedding guests filling the wedding hall, ready for the great celebration for his Bride and Groom.

Time Block 7A

However, a guest stands out. Did you notice the King addresses this person as "Friend"?

The King is kind and asks a simple question; where are your wedding clothes? The guest is speechless, which is his downfall. He has nothing to say, not a single word to attempt to explain.

Think about the following:

1. This man was an invited guest to the wedding between the Bride (followers of Christ) and the Groom (Jesus)
2. Both good and bad people were invited
3. The King calls him "Friend"

But, he is thrown into the Outer Darkness (not the Lake of Fire though, note that).

This man has intrigued me for a very long time, and you'll find many answers as to what it means. However, let us look simply at this again: many receive invites to the wedding feast as *guests*, and not as the Bride. Indeed, Jesus was telling this parable to the leaders of the Jewish faith, to show them the truth of how they had treated the Prophets and even God himself.

The very fact that this man without wedding clothes is thrown into the Outer Darkness, also points to him being of the Jewish faith—as Matthew 8:11-12 tells us:

> And I tell you this, that many Gentiles will come from all over the world—from east and west—and sit down with Abraham, Isaac, and Jacob at the feast in the Kingdom of Heaven. But many Israelites—those for whom the Kingdom was prepared—will be thrown into outer darkness, where there will be weeping and gnashing of teeth. NLT

It therefore must follow that he is one of God's Chosen people—the Israelites. Good and bad, they receive the invite to the wedding party of Jesus to his followers (Christians, Tribulation Saints etc.) as God intends to save all of Israel, as mentioned before. How then, did the guest come to have no wedding clothes?

It would seem either he refused to do what is required (he rejected Jesus as Christ his savior) or he thought he would follow his own desires and dress in whatever he wanted to (in self-important pride). These are definite ways to the Outer Darkness, if you are a chosen one.

A Quick Note on Damnation

God never built the Lake of Fire to destroy human souls, rather it is reserved for Satan and his angels (i.e., messengers). If you want a Bible reference that states this, remember the Sheep and Goats: see Matthew 25:41:

> "Then he will say to those on his left, 'Depart from me, you cursed, into the eternal fire prepared for the devil and his angels.'" ESV

God wants everyone to come (freely) to the New Heavens and the New Earth and live with him in peace. However, people full of pride and bitterness will damn themselves and side with Satan, and perhaps even become those messengers. It is a terrible truth; it shows even with the removal of doubt that Jesus exists during the 1 000-year reign (because he is there in front of the whole world at that time), a certain human nature will always reject God's authority. After all, an army comes up against Jesus in Time Block 6B, so that's a lot of people (possibly those Goats) rejecting him!

With those insisting to be damned through rejecting the free ticket out, God then has no choice but to follow his rule—*nothing* unholy can enter the New Heavens and New Earth. Nothing! It is devoid of such things forever. And how does anyone become holy if we are all unholy, each and every one of us? By Jesus declaring us as his, taking on our un-holiness upon himself and wiping our own slate clean.

Furthermore, the only *other* things left in existence are the Lake of Fire and the Outer Darkness. There is nowhere else to go. There is no old Earth or old spacetime left for others to live in. Simply put, with humanity's souls now in eternal bodies, the choices are therefore: God's new creation, Lake of Fire or Outer Darkness as per Time Block 7B to come.

To those who bemoan it is unfair that they should have to face eternity suffering in an immortal body they never asked for, and would prefer the notion of just disappearing—consider the following:

If you accept one of God's multiple offers of free salvation along the way, and your emotional need is to be unaware (go out like a light) for eternity, Jesus promises us *all* our emotional needs as our Husband, signed by contract, in his blood. Therefore, if you want nothing to do with Heaven, the destruction of the Second Death or the suffering of the Outer Darkness, then choose Jesus as your Lord. Then, when you have your own eternal body, you can ask him to be unconscious as your emotional need. See? To reject him and hope you "go out like a light" is foolish and such a big gamble.

Time Block 7 A

In a broad summary: God invited people through the Prophets that spoke in the Old Testament; then through the free gift of Jesus's sacrifice and the giving of the Holy Spirit. Next, through the truth of the Two Witnesses that prophesy against the Beast; then from the teaching of the 144 000 and 1 000 years of Holy and Truthful rule from God himself in Jesus on the Earth, without Satan. That's a long invite, full of sacrifice and patience by God. All poured out for us. We just have to say yes please. However, people don't and won't. We see this now as I write this; we will see it in the future until it is too late.

Who Does the Judging?

Another important point is: who does the judging? Many times as I grew up, I saw images, films, and so on that showed The Father as the judge. But this is not biblically accurate! Jesus tells us with his own lips in John 5:22, 26–27 that the Father judges no one:

> For the Father judges no one, but has given all judgment to the Son, that all may honor the Son, just as they honor the Father . . .
> . . . For as the Father has life in himself, so he has granted the Son also to have life in himself. And he has given him authority to execute judgment, because he is the Son of Man." ᴱˢⱽ

The Son has been granted absolute authority to judge, doing his Father's will.

This reinforces the idea Jesus told us: he is the door, the gateway to the fold—that no one comes to the Father except through him (Jesus). Every single soul that has ever existed in our creation has to stand before Jesus and be granted, on his authority and holy judgment, to proceed to the New Heaven and New Earth, or be thrown out. That is clear.

Judgment Process

We can see the nature of the Judgment Process in Revelation 20:12–13:

> I saw the dead, both great and small, standing before God's throne. And the books were opened, including the Book of Life. And the dead were judged according to what they had done, as recorded in the books. The sea gave up its dead, and death and the grave gave up their dead. And all were judged according to their deeds. ᴺᴸᵀ

There seems to be clear distinction here of Book of Life and "Deeds." Now all Christians will tell you rightly that we, as Christ's flock and his Bride, avoid judgment as we have humbly accepted God's perfect sacrifice for us in the Lamb of Jesus. We are in the Book of Life, and Jesus will declare us *his* in front of the Father. We have a ticket given to us by God that cannot be taken away.

But, what of those who never knew Jesus? Like the millions of people who died not knowing scripture, not ever knowing the Holy Spirit (as he was only poured out on us after Jesus's Resurrection and Ascension)? Or those never existing in a Christian society, including what remains after the Beast Kingdom?

What I have understood from the Holy Spirit and Bible is as I mentioned before: every single person has, and had, God teaching them his law on their heart leading them to Jesus the shepherd, convicted through their own thoughts, as per Romans 2:12-16. Paul in Acts 17:22-31 alludes to this. Here is vs 27:

> "His purpose was for the nations to seek after God and perhaps feel their way toward him and find him—though he is not far from any one of us." NLT

We know Jesus is the *only* gate to the kingdom, to his fold, the narrow path and the way; but that does not negate him having the choice of who to let in of those who never knew him. He is both the door and the fold. He is the Gate and the Good Shepherd.

Beware all those who then think: "Hey! Free ride, I just have to be a good person." No! Because there is no one "good," we all deserve judgment—both Isaiah 53:6 and Romans 3:23-24 make this clear:

Isaiah 53:6:

> All of us, like sheep, have strayed away. We have left God's paths to follow our own. Yet the Lord laid on him the sins of us all. NLT

Romans 3:23-24:

> For everyone has sinned; we all fall short of God's glorious standard. Yet God, in his grace, freely makes us right in his sight. He did this through Christ Jesus when he freed us from the penalty for our sins. NLT

If you have heard of, or know Jesus, and then reject him wholeheartly—then you are not in the Book of Life. If you are reading this study, you have a chance to begin to know of Jesus. You have enough information about him to know what you have to do. So, read the Gospels of Matthew, Mark, Luke, and John and come to know him in your heart.

The kind of people I am talking about are the *never heard of Jesus*. Those who die as babies or young children. Those who die in remote areas, never visited by the Word of God in the Bible. Those kept away from him by violence and oppression, or teachings, through no fault of their own.

These will rise to the resurrection of judgment as Jesus told us, to be judged righteously by Jesus the gateway, perhaps by the Law the Father wrote on their hearts and their acceptance of it, knowingly or unknowingly, like the sheep and goats.

It has to follow, therefore, that the sheep Jesus separates from the goats in Matthew 25:31–46 are then written into the Lamb's Book of Life, as I will explain in the following heading.

In a way, rejection of Jesus (Father, Holy Spirit) is the way to the Lake of Fire or the Outer Darkness. Philosophically, how is it possible to reject someone you never knew of?

Second Timothy 2:11–13 points us to this idea of rejecting. See how denying him is the only way he denies us:

> The saying is trustworthy, for:
> If we have died with him, we will also live with him;
> If we endure, we will also reign with him;
> If we deny him, he also will deny us;
> If we are faithless, he remains faithful—for he cannot deny himself. ESV

How do you deny someone? By *knowing* them, *who they are*, and consciously choosing *not* to allow them to be that. Think of "self-denial" and what that means. Now think of "Jesus denial." It is the same concept.

The Book of Life is the Key

After all I said previously about judgment by Jesus our Lord, the best thing to remember is simply this: All those not found in The Lamb's (Jesus's) Book of Life are cast into the Lake of Fire with Satan, his angels, the Beast, and the Antichrist.

That's a very top-level view of the judgment and one that is very, very simple to understand. If I am wrong about those who never knew Jesus, I am certainly *not* wrong about the Book of Life. That is as clear-cut as it gets.

Everything else—the "other books opened," the sheep and goats—must culminate in your name in or out of the final Book of Life.

It doesn't matter what you believe about fairness, babies, free will vs predestination, animal souls, no hell just oblivion, and so on: if your name is *not* in the Book of Life, you *are* in the Lake of Fire. End of discussion. The Word of God has made it that simple to understand.

Therefore, the most important part of this whole study for you, a conscious being capable of free will and thought is: *do you know how to ensure you are in the Book of Life?* And do you understand how to avoid having your name blotted out by Jesus? Here's a clear message spoken by Jesus in John 5:24:

> "Truly, truly, I say to you, whoever hears my word and believes him who sent me has eternal life. He does not come into judgment, but has passed from death to life." ESV

So remember, accepting Christ as your savior, listening to him and repenting of your fallen sin nature is a sure-fire way into his book.

Timeline Segment Summary: Time Block 7A

For a deeper study of the final Day of the Lord, the end of our spacetime and everyone's final judgment, take a read of the following Bible verses:

* The end of our spacetime creation: Psalm 102:25–27, Hebrews 12:27, 2 Peter 3:7–13, Revelation 20:11, Revelation 21:1
* Don't delude yourself: Isaiah 28:14–22, John 9:39–41, John 15:22–25, Acts 17:22–31, Hebrews 12:25
* Everyone will get a resurrection body: 1 Corinthians 15:22, 1 Corinthians 15:35–58, Hebrews 12:22–29, Revelation 20:5 (2nd sentence)
* The manner of judgment: Matthew 22:11–14, Matthew 25:31–46, Mark 4:22–23, John 12:44–50, Revelation 20:12–13
* The Lamb's Book of Life is the key: Revelation 3:3–5, Revelation 13:8, Revelation 20:15, Revelation 21:27
* Death is destroyed (for everyone): Isaiah 25:8, 1 Corinthians 15:26, Revelation 20:14–15
* The fallen angels are also judged: 2 Peter 2:4, Jude 6

Time Block 7B

Eternity: Revelation 21, Revelation 22

The Time Block Overview											
The End Begins	Rise of the Modern World	Jesus Revealed [Day of the LORD]		The Three Terrors				Jesus Returns [Day of the LORD]		1 000-Year Reign		Judgment [Day of the LORD] and New Creation
1	2		3		4				5		6		7
A	A	B	A	B	A	B	C	D	E	A	B	A	B	A	B

The End.
The Start of Eternity.

Eternal Epilogue

How I wish I could write " . . . and the entirety of Humanity lived happily ever after."

But the truth is: it will not be all of us, for the path is narrow and our stubborn human pride is huge and unwieldy. I am a saved Christian, given salvation through Grace alone, and bathed in the Holy Spirit as a wonderful free and undeserved gift; and yet every day I have to fight my own pride and underlying base personality that is far from blameless. It is an endless battle against me, me, and me. John the Baptist understood this: he said that he had to decrease as Christ increases. It is the same today for anyone. We must decrease to the point of total selflessness like Christ did, which is very hard to do indeed, and I would suggest without God's help it is impossible.

At this point in our Time Block journey, the saved, redeemed, sorted, and chosen are now living in the New Creation (a new spacetime as it were) side by side with God. They are in new, amazing bodies, healed by the Tree of Life (the one that was in the center of Eden). The River of Life replenishes them, and their symbolic husband Jesus, meets all their emotional needs.

No More Sin

One of the remarkable effects of this new creation, and the new bodies based on the sinless pattern of the New Adam Jesus (i.e., God in Physical Form), is the removal of the corruption from that original sin brought about by Satan. Indeed, Satan has gone forever. Without his devastating influence on us, and only the pure influence of Jesus, we might *just* imagine a distant glimpse of what it will be like. I suspect some people will be thinking "a life of goodie-two-shoes where you can't be naughty – oh *great*." Perhaps a better way of thinking of it is "oh a life of loving kindness, trust, honesty, excitement, and nothing to worry us anymore." Revelation 21:3-4 also gives us an idea of what that eternity will look like:

> I heard a loud shout from the throne, saying, "Look, God's home is now among his people! He will live with them, and they will be his people. God himself will be with them. He will wipe every tear from their eyes, and there will be no more death or sorrow or crying or pain. All these things are gone forever." NLT

Lake of Fire (Second Death) and Outer Darkness

As mentioned before—I noticed two distinct endings for those who don't make it to the New Jerusalem in the New Heavens and Earth.

Firstly, there is the easy to understand Lake of Fire to destroy immortal fallen angels—or demons as we call them. Unfortunately, there will be resurrected human souls in there too. This is the Western idea of Hell, with the difference from the Bible that nothing in there has any power structure to rule over others and no servants to do their bidding, just simple eternal destruction.

The other place is the Outer Darkness where there is wailing and gnashing of teeth. This seems to suggest deep mourning from the societal context at the time. Only the Gospel of Matthew mentions this outer darkness, and Jesus seemingly aimed this idea firstly at the Jewish leaders (Pharisees and Scribes he calls hypocrites in Matthew 23), and secondly as a warning about servants that act lazily or wickedly. Who are these servants? Read following passages and work out what the Holy Spirit is saying:

> Matthew 24:48-51:
> But what if the servant is evil and thinks, "My master won't be back for a while," and he begins beating the other servants, partying, and getting drunk? The master will return unannounced and unexpected, and he will cut the servant to pieces and assign him a place with the hypocrites. In that place there will be weeping and gnashing of teeth. NLT

> Matthew 25:29-30:
> "To those who use well what they are given, even more will be given, and they will have an abundance. But from those who do nothing, even what little they have will be taken away. Now throw this useless servant into outer darkness, where there will be weeping and gnashing of teeth." NLT

Always remember the 100 percent basic truth: if your name is in the Book of Life, you will avoid both options. So get your name into that book, and keep it in there.

Who Wants Eternity? It'll be *Boring*!

One of the issues my son had at the time of writing (and I often have considered this myself) is: won't we be bored out of our minds with monotony and repetition? You know, the same old happiness day in day out for millions and millions of years? Surely Eternity = Eventual Boredom, right?

Well, I suspect the continuous mental disappointment we have now, in this creation, is non-existent in the new. After all, Jesus signed a marriage contract in his blood that says he will look after us for eternity. Surely, if we find ourselves chewing our nails and absent mindedly picking fluff off our white garments, he'd be there and ask, "what is wrong"? "I'm bored," we'd say, sighing. And then, what do you think God would do for you? Say "deal with it" and walk off whistling a merry tune? Tell you that perhaps you should do some drawing? Like on a rainy day stuck inside the house as young children? Or, do you think he'd tend to your emotional *needs* and ensure your new eternal life does not contain the notion of boredom?

We have a hard concept with eternity because we live in a decaying, fallen world where tastes become bland and new becomes old. Entropy reigns all around us. We count the passing years. Most experiences or objects seem to be not as good as they were before. So how can we imagine a place where the reverse is true and there are new blessings each day? C.S.Lewis tried to illustrate this as declaring Heaven as a book that gets better with each chapter, and never ends. This is probably as best an analogy we can imagine: interest and excitement, new and better *forever*.

Of course, there is the rather harder concept to grasp that fits nicely with God the Father. There will be no time as we know it. Time in its normal sense is actually an invention of mankind to explain how long something took to pass. What we actually live in is an intrinsically linked space and time called spacetime. If you wish to learn more, read Stephen Hawking's interesting book "A Brief History of Time,"[1] especially chapter nine where Dr. Hawking explains our fundamental view of the constant march of time.

When we consider what Jesus could do in his glorified New Adam body, we start to get a glimpse of what non-ordinary time would look like. In the passages of Luke 24:35–43, Jesus appears amongst his hiding disciples in an instant, and proves he has a solid body by eating some fish. Therefore, it took *zero time* to manifest his presence, but took *some time* to talk and eat fish. That is not ordinary as we know and experience life.

Therefore, looking at Jesus's physical body and capabilities, we need to understand eternity in the same manner. We'll become multi-dimensional beings where time is meaningless, but seemingly still existing. For instance, the Tree of Life (coming up later in this study) bears fruit every month. It follows therefore that we could measure and understand a month if desired.

Going back to the original point—boredom. How can you be bored if the concept of passing time can be non-existent if you so choose? One prayer from our lips could last a pico-second or for an eternity.

If eternity lasts an instant, how could you get bored? And if an instant lasts an eternity, how can you grasp that concept?

New Heavens, New Earth, and New Jerusalem

Another philosophical problem with Heaven being constant happiness and joy for eternity is this: if there is only joy, and no reference point of sadness, then what is joy? Endless joy becomes the normal state, which becomes

---

1. Hawking, Stephen (1988). *A Brief History of Time*.

meaningless for there isn't anything else. However, just like the Western world has distorted Hell to be a place where you can serve Satan and be a demon in his domain, so our view of Heaven has likewise been distorted.

There is work to be done in the New Heavens and the New Earth, and our apprenticeship in this current creation will lead us to be masters of our purpose in the New Creation.

Therefore, it is likely we will still have a range of emotions as we go about our purposeful work, so that we will still understand what Joy is, and what Sadness is.

In Revelation 21 we get a description of the new creation. Interestingly, John notes that the sea is no more. Why that is, I have no guidance to offer and I am disappointed by that idea, on this side of Eternity, in Old Adam-based reality. I am sure we will all see the folly of this disappointment when we are actually there. There are some ideas that the sea symbolically stood for chaos, so that could mean chaos is no more.

There is also a New Jerusalem coming down out of the New Heavens from God. This new city is described as a Bride of the Lamb, with the joy, beauty, and happiness the Jewish people would understand in context of the times John was writing. As you read about this city, you'll discover it is a cube! Quite a gigantic cube in fact. And interestingly, you'll notice that in this new creation there are nations and Kings that come up and bring their honor and glory into the city. However, only those whose name is in that Lamb's Book of Life can enter.

This leads to an interesting concept: a formation of a whole new sinless creation, in which nations freely move about and the Book of Life people can come and go from the huge cube-like New Jerusalem. In this New Jerusalem resides The Lord God Almighty (The Father) and the Lamb (Jesus) as visibly separate entities that are indeed One God. It therefore follows that the third Person of the single God must also be there, as God is eternal and does not change. Perhaps the water of life that flows from God's throne and nourishes the Tree of Life in Revelation 22 describes the Holy Spirit symbolically?

The Tree of Life

Way back at the start of the journey with God, in Genesis 2:9, we read about the Garden of Eden. Right in the midst of this was the Tree of Life, along with the Tree of Knowledge of Good and Evil.

Adam, and later Eve, could freely eat from the Tree of Life as well as all the other trees, with the exception of one. The tree that caused our downfall and tainted our DNA, was the Tree of Knowledge of Good and Evil—for before we were without knowledge, and therefore could not sin.

After Adam and Eve eat that forbidden fruit, God then says to all his aspects:

> "Behold, the man has become like one of Us in knowing good and evil. Now, lest he reach out his hand and take also from the Tree of Life, and eat, and live forever." ESV

It is after this that God then banishes Adam and Eve from the Garden of Eden and places mighty guardian cherubim and a flaming sword to protect the Tree of Life.

Notice we were in grave danger of becoming *immortal sinning* creatures if we could still access the Tree of Life.

From this sad event, a price had to be paid to reverse that embedded trickery by Satan, which is still passed from parent to child in every Old Adam-based human.

So, Jesus came as Son of Man, Son of God, and became the Lamb of God to provide the perfect sacrifice for us all. He is also the New Adam, so that those who believe in him might at last eat from that Tree of Life and live eternally—but now as sinless creatures instead based on the New Adam bodies.

Revelation 22 describes the Tree of Life as having leaves that heal the Nations, as well as a fresh crop of fruits each month. Given that God states that the Tree of Life provides eternal life (as above), the fruits must also be for the new resurrected bodies as eternal nourishment; as we will be physical beings, we can literally eat them just as Jesus ate fish with the disciples on a couple of occasions.

What happened when Adam and Eve could no longer eat from the fruits of the Tree of Life? The Bible states that Adam continued to live for 930 years (Genesis 5:5). So, although he no longer had access to the healing and lifegiving fruits, it would seem the effect on his body lasted a very, very long time. Indeed, even his offspring had very long lives for the most part.

Time Block 7B

Timeline Segment Summary: Time Block 7B

And finally, you have come to the epilogue of eternity in Heaven, or the Lake of Fire and the Outer Darkness. You have just a few more passages to study for the End of the World:

* Living with God for Eternity: Psalm 23:6, Ephesians 2:19–22, Revelation 21:3–4 & 6–7
* A New Creation (new spacetime?): Isaiah 65:17, 2 Peter 3:13, Revelation 21:1–2, 5
* A new, immense Jerusalem: Isaiah 62:2–5, Revelation 3:12 (2nd and 3rd sentences), Revelation 21:10–26
* The Tree of Life: Genesis 2:9, Genesis 3:22–24, Revelation 2:7, Revelation 22:1–2, 14, 19
* Lake of Fire (the Second Death): Revelation 2:11, Revelation 14:9–11, Revelation 20:10 and 15, Revelation 21:8
* Outer Darkness: Matthew 8:10–12, Matthew 22:13, Matthew 24:50–51, Matthew 25:30

Conclusion

What to do and Where are We?

To recap, here are some conclusions to be drawn from the study I have presented.

Firstly, without a doubt, you can avoid a lot of disaster and tribulation by focusing on the truth: be a Bride of Christ, reading words of Jesus in the Bible, accepting his salvation, asking for forgiveness please, and agreeing with his declaration that he is God, as inseparable from The Father and Holy Spirit as you are from your soul and spirit. You won't avoid all disaster in your life, but you are *guaranteed* to have your name in the Book of Life. That, my friend, is the most important thing you'll do on this planet.

Secondly, the height of the Beast's mouthpiece, his physical appearance, his name, what his favorite color is, etc. matters as much as a passing fly on a windy day. What matters is you recognize *where* you are in the timeline (I am in the Time Block 2B on page 28) and never, ever, ever, accept the Beast's mark on your hand or forehead or heart. For those people that do accept, they have a direct line to the Lake of Fire. It truly is better to die at the hands of the Beast's henchmen and suffer a short destruction than to suffer an eternal destruction that never ends. I hope you never exist in those times for it is truly terrible.

Thirdly, I think the rapture theory has very good evidence, and it would seem I am a pre- to midtribulation rapturist. Why do I say that? Because I definitely believe the Bride will be removed before the terrible destruction of Time Block 3B and the Terrors when the Destroyer reigns; but the Bride will be here to experience the beginnings of Revelation 6:4–9, in that we will experience terrible times of famine, hyper-inflation, widespread war, along with unstoppable disease and death by wild animals. Therefore, although Christians want to look forwards to the Rapture, I personally would

Conclusion

rather die a natural death *before* that time and not have to go through the tribulations beforehand. Remember Jesus's messenger (Angel) tells us the multitude *come out of* a tribulation.

Fourthly, it is not a leap of imagination to see how very close we are to Time Block 3A, the Revealing of Christ. At the time of writing I am amazed to witness the rebirth of nuclear war as a distinct possibility. In case this is all a memory again—it began with in the early part of 2018 with the ever-increasing North Korean Nuclear Missile Tests and President Donald Trump of the USA performing brinkmanship. Next, President Putin invaded Ukraine in 2022, and has repeatedly made comments about using nuclear missiles if NATO interferes too much. Meanwhile, China bides its time watching the outcomes.

We all know that if a nuclear weapon is used, we have a big issue in global economy: cue hyperinflation, cue panic, cue warfare. Ten or so years before 2022, the threat of nuclear war was truly a memory; it is amazing how fast it can become brinkmanship and saber waving at the cost of eight billion people's future!

In terms of disease: in early 2020 we began the global spread of COVID 19, which although not as deadly as some diseases, managed to crash stock markets and greatly affected people's livelihoods.

Considering what we've experienced with the societal cost of COVID, how much worse would a pandemic of smallpox style virus be today? Smallpox killed approximately three out of ten people who contracted it.[1] As a comparison, COVID 19 has a death rate of approximately two people out of every *one hundred* who contract it.[2] Therefore COVID 19 is approximately ten times less deadly than smallpox. Yet this slow burner pandemic has created great social divides, violence, remarkable misinformation, and collapse of trust; not to mention the effect on economies with inflation, and small businesses with loss of income.

Lastly, take a moment to look around at the Western World that a lot of the developing world aspires to be. It's all shiny and comfortable right? So long as you keep the beggars off the streets, remove the homeless from their camps so we don't notice them, and don't look at your debt. Oh, and ignore the accepted over-use of sex and drugs for leisure and entertainment (and yes that includes alcohol as this is a mind altering drug as anyone who

---

1. Centers for Disease Control and Prevention, *History of Smallpox*.

2. https://www.worldometers.info/coronavirus/#countries, figures from deaths, recoveries and total case – August 25, 2021

drinks it can attest). Splendid! If the whole world manages to reach our level, then we have the perfect timing for Jesus to come back and begin the clean-up.

Just remember—death by wild animals on a large scale is the only part of Revelation 6:4–9 we have not yet seen in our history up to now. If you ever see this, surely time is short.

A Final Word

I am fully convinced I was led to all the Bible passages to create the original timeline, from which the Time Blocks formed. Some of those passages I deleted after re-re-rechecking as confidence was not high.

Most of what I have explained is how I have understood the Holy Spirit's inspiration, coupled with a sanity check with my pastor who guided me with the three types of prophecy. The parts that are just my thoughts I have tried my best to highlight that they are my thoughts, and therefore bear no weight.

Also read James 3:1—a warning to people like me, who would teach the Bible. If we ask the Holy Spirit for wisdom, and we have a desire to lead others to that wisdom, we had better do it with care and love, and do what Jesus wants us to do with that wisdom. People who teach the Bible are setting themselves up for stricter judgment and rightly so. With that warning in mind, I am full of prayer, humilty, and care that I have not mislead or spoken falsehoods, and have walked carefully through the depths of the Bible vs the world influence.

Please help me Lord Jesus be truthful to your Word. Amen

Conclusion

Here is a condensed review of the seven major Time Blocks, for your quick reference.

Time Block	Summary	Notes
1	The End Times Begin	This is the birth, death and resurrection of Jesus. The start of the end.
2	Rise of the Modern World	Jesus departs and gifts the Holy Spirit as a promise he will be back. The modern world grows to what we have in the twenty-first century.
3	Jesus Revealed	Jesus is revealed to everyone, and collects his bride as promised. The Black Sun/Red Moon event signifies the end of the modern way.
4	The Terrors	Terrible destruction of all societies. From this rises the new and final world order: The Beast Kingdom. The terrors end with the mighty angelic and earthly battle.
5	Jesus the Messiah Returns	Jesus returns as the Messiah, the conquering king, with all his angels and servants (including the Bride). Defeats the Beast Kingdom completely. The Darkened Sun/Darkened Moon event signifies this powerful day.
6	The Millenial Reign of the Messiah	Jesus reigns on Earth from the third temple in Jerusalem. Satan is imprisoned for this duration, then released and destroyed at the end.
7	Final Judgement and Eternity	All spacetime is melted, and everyone faces Jesus to be judged by the Lamb's Book of Life. This leads to an eternity cherished by God or damned to the Lake of Fire or Outer Darkness.

Appendix A

Do You Know Jesus?

The Bible describes Jesus in many ways throughout history, and into the future and the end. Here are his many attributes and differing manifestations:

* As John says in his gospel, Jesus was first the "Word of God," and he was with God from the beginning and was God. All things were created through him, for him.
* Then, Jesus became the "New Adam" (man), "Son of God," "Son of Man," who walked among us, teaching us and showing the truth of what God was like, and how we could have a relationship with God.
* He then became the "Lamb of God," savior and redeemer of all; being the perfect sacrifice required to fulfill the old Law and to free us from slavery to sin.
* Then Jesus was the "Groom," returning alive to his Father to wait and prepare a place for his bride, and to leave the beautiful gift of the Holy Spirit. He will appear once more as the Groom, to gather the Bride into his household and return to Heaven.
* Next, Jesus will return as the mighty conqueror "The Messiah"—the one the Jewish people are waiting for, to rule on the Earth as King of Kings and save them all. He will sit on his throne in the Temple and vanquish all evil and Satan.
* When that is complete, Jesus will become the perfect "Judge," the "Gateway" and the "Sheep Fold" into the New Heavens and Earth. We will all meet and see him, and be judged completely fairly and fully righteously.

Appendix A

* Finally, for eternity, Jesus will be a perfect, caring "Companion" to those who did not reject him; God as an intertwined being with our own immortal and new glorified bodies and souls. Walking with us and looking after us in love forevermore.

As you can see, Jesus is indeed a complex person.

Appendix B

Who is the "I AM"?

For Westerners who know English, if someone asked you your name and you smiled and said, "I am who I am" I'm quite sure you'd get odd looks. Some translations have that quotation as "I am that I am."

However, God uses this title way, way back in Moses's day when he speaks to Moses from the burning bush in Exodus 3:14. It is an odd thing to say. In the end he tells Moses to say to the people "I AM has sent me to you."

This ancient message caused the Jewish leaders facing Jesus to become angrily surprised and shocked when Jesus said that he was "I AM."

Furthermore, in Exodus 3:15, God tells Moses that this is his name (God's) forever.

So who is "I AM"? He is Jesus, the Father, and the Spirit. One God, in three parts as described on page 2. We can even see this in the very first passages of the Bible:

Genesis 1:1:

> "In the beginning, God created the heavens and the earth." ESV

This is the Father, who we can't grasp mentally or physically as he is so unusual and not of this spacetime we understand, but created all that in which we reside.

Genesis 1:2:

> "The earth was without form and void, and darkness was over the face of the deep. And the Spirit of God was hovering over the face of the waters." ESV

Clearly this is the Holy Spirit, not bound to the Father, but free to be in and through our spacetime as he sees fit.

Appendix B

Genesis 1:3:

"And God said, 'Let there be light,' and there was light." ᴱˢⱽ

God spoke. Do you know who the Word of God is? John tells us in John 1:14 that the Word of God became flesh and dwelt amongst us. He was there at the beginning and is indeed Jesus. The same Word of God that spoke to Moses and said: "I AM who I AM." Jesus even tells the Jewish leaders that he existed long, long ago as God in the powerful passages of John 8:31–59 if you would like to read that.

So, there you have it: God the one and only God displaying how to be three separate Persons in the very first few sentences of the Bible. Lovely.

Bibliography

AICE, https://www.jewishvirtuallibrary.org/marriage-in-judaism, see heading "*A Typical Ashkenazi Wedding Ceremony*"

Boston Dynamics, *Introducing Handle*, Feb 27, 2017, https://www.youtube.com/watch?v=-7xvqQeoA8c

Centers for Disease Control and Prevention, *History of Smallpox*, https://www.cdc.gov/smallpox/history/history.html

Flavius Josephus, *Of the War – Book VII, Chapter 1*. Translated by William Whiston, M.A. https://penelope.uchicago.edu/josephus/war-7.html

Hawking, Stephen. *A Brief History of Time*. Bantam Books, 1988

Wikipedia, *Abomination of Desolation*, https://en.wikipedia.org/wiki/abomination_of_desolation. See headings '*Rabbinical Literature*' and '*Multiple Fulfilments*'

Wikipedia, *Isaiah Scroll*, https://en.m.wikipedia.org/wiki/Isaiah_Scroll

Wikipedia, *Jewish Wedding*, https://en.wikipedia.org/wiki/Jewish_wedding#Yichud

Wikipedia, *Third Temple*, https://en.m.wikipedia.org/wiki/third_temple. See heading "*Jewish Views*"

www.ingramcontent.com/pod-product-compliance
Lightning Source LLC
Chambersburg PA
CBHW060821190426
43197CB00038B/2179